Athlete Burnout

Athlete Burnout: Recognition, Prevention, and Management provides the first contemporary account of athlete burnout. Drawing on academic literature from both inside and outside of sport, this book focuses on providing the tools necessary to understand and recognise the symptoms of athlete burnout. It also informs practice by providing evidence-based intervention strategies to aid in the prevention and management of athlete burnout.

Written in a concise, user-friendly, and accessible format for athletes and coaches, this book provides novel insights for practitioners, students, and academics alike interested in athlete health and sport psychology.

Daniel J. Madigan is a Professor of Sport and Health Psychology at York St John University, UK. His research focuses on the predictors, consequences, and prevention of burnout in various achievement contexts. He has produced over 100 peer-reviewed journal articles and book chapters in this area. He holds Accreditation with the Chartered Association of Sport and Exercise Sciences and has previously served as Editor of the *International Journal of Sport Psychology*.

Henrik Gustafsson is a Professor of Sport Science at Karlstad University, Sweden, and a Visiting Professor at the Norwegian School of Sport Science. His research focuses on burnout in sport. He has published more than 100 peer-reviewed journal articles and book chapters in this area. He is an accredited sport psychologist and has supported Swedish national athletes at three Olympic Games and serves as a Sector Editor of the *Scandinavian Journal of Medicine and Science in Sports*.

Luke F. Olsson is a Senior Lecturer in Sport Psychology at Liverpool John Moores University, UK. His research focuses on vulnerabilities and consequences of athlete burnout. He has published numerous peer-reviewed journal articles and book chapters in this area. He is a graduate member of the British Psychological Society and serves as an Associate Editor of *Anxiety, Stress, and Coping*.

J.D. DeFreese is a Teaching Associate Professor at the University of North Carolina at Chapel Hill, USA. His research focuses on the motivational and psychosocial predictors of athlete burnout and athlete transition out of sport. He has published over 80 peer-reviewed journal articles and book chapters in these areas. He edited a recent special issue on burnout in sport in the *Journal of Clinical Sport Psychology* for which he also serves as an Associate Editor.

Routledge Psychology of Sport, Exercise and Physical Activity

Series Editor: Andrew M. Lane
University of Wolverhampton, UK

This series offers a forum for original and cutting-edge research exploring the latest ideas and issues in the psychology of sport, exercise and physical activity. Books within the series showcase the work of well-established and emerging scholars from around the world, offering an international perspective on topical and emerging areas of interest in the field. This series aims to drive forward academic debate and bridge the gap between theory and practice, encouraging critical thinking and reflection among students, academics and practitioners. The series is aimed at upper-level undergraduates, research students and academics, and contains both authored and edited collections.

The Psychology of Closed Self-Paced Motor Tasks in Sports
Edited by Ronnie Lidor and Gal Ziv

Passion and Addiction in Sports and Exercise
Attila Szabo and Zsolt Demetrovics

Decision Making for Sports Officials
Training and Assessment Perspectives
Ian Cunningham, Aden Kittel, Duncan Mascarenhas, Clare MacMahon, and Paul Larkin

Athlete Burnout
Recognition, Prevention, and Management
Daniel J. Madigan, Henrik Gustafsson, Luke F. Olsson, and J.D. DeFreese

For more information about this series, please visit: https://www.routledge.com/Routledge-Psychology-of-Sport-Exercise-and-Physical-Activity/book-series/RRSP

Athlete Burnout

Recognition, Prevention, and Management

Daniel J. Madigan, Henrik Gustafsson, Luke F. Olsson, and J.D. DeFreese

Routledge
Taylor & Francis Group
NEW YORK AND LONDON

First published 2026
by Routledge
605 Third Avenue, New York, NY 10158

and by Routledge
4 Park Square, Milton Park, Abingdon, Oxon, OX14 4RN

Routledge is an imprint of the Taylor & Francis Group, an informa business

ISBN: 978-1-032-98538-1 (hbk)
ISBN: 978-1-032-98874-0 (pbk)
ISBN: 978-1-003-60109-8 (ebk)

DOI: 10.4324/9781003601098

Typeset in Sabon
by KnowledgeWorks Global Ltd.

For Huxley

Contents

List of Figures and Tables *x*
Preface *xi*

1 Recognising the Symptoms of Athlete Burnout 1

2 Reviewing the Consequences of Athlete Burnout 11

3 Preventing Athlete Burnout 26

4 Intervening to Manage Athlete Burnout 41

5 Considering the Future of Athlete Burnout 60

Index *70*

Figures and Tables

Figures

1.1 Changes in average athlete burnout symptoms over time 7
3.1 Overview of perfectionism-athlete burnout theory 32

Tables

1.1 Symptoms, example items, and response format for determining the frequency of burnout symptoms 4
2.1 Summary of the possible consequences of athlete burnout and the evidence to support each relationship 21
4.1 Studies examining interventions to reduce athlete burnout 44
4.2 Recommendations for therapies to help reduce athlete burnout 49

Preface

Supporting athlete mental health is one of the highest priorities for those working in sport (Vella et al., 2021). The demands on athletes, however, only continue to grow. As they do so, athlete mental health becomes more at risk. The difficulties that athletes face are reflected in the fact that athletes display comparable or even higher levels of mental health problems, such as depression and anxiety, than the general population (e.g., Nicholls et al., 2020; Nixdorf et al., 2013; Purcell et al., 2020). In addition, they experience problems unique to their sport participation. One highly salient factor is athlete burnout. Burnout not only hinders athletic performance but also underpins athletes' decisions to leave sport altogether (Gustafsson et al., 2017). Worryingly, reflecting increased pressures to perform, recent evidence highlights that athlete burnout is on the rise, and has been for the past two decades (Madigan et al., 2022).

This book is about understanding why athlete burnout is at an all-time high, and, importantly, what can be done by those involved in sport to reverse this trend. We think now is an opportune time to do so. This is because the scientific study of athlete burnout as a field has reached a level of maturity whereby there is much empirical work to inform our recommendations and to warrant the first book on this topic. Consequently, in the following five chapters, we aim to provide the theoretical and empirical basis for understanding and overcoming athlete burnout.

In Chapter 1, we aim to provide the necessary basics to understand burnout. This includes defining what athlete burnout is and examining the tools that are available to measure it. We also discuss possible ways to practically monitor burnout symptoms. The chapter ends with a discussion of the evidence and reasons underpinning the increasing prevalence of athlete burnout.

In Chapter 2, we review the literature examining the consequences of athlete burnout. In doing so, we outline the reasons why we should be so concerned about increasing rates of athlete burnout.

In Chapter 3, we provide an overview of theoretical explanations of burnout development. We then use this information as the means to develop strategies to help prevent athlete burnout.

In Chapter 4, we review interventions for reducing burnout. This includes a large body of literature outside of sport and also, in more detail, studies that have specifically focused on athletes. In this chapter, we provide detailed practical recommendations for those working with athletes.

In the final chapter, Chapter 5, we end with a discussion of what is next for the field. We discuss opinion pieces in recently published special issues on athlete burnout. In doing so, we highlight what leading researchers in the area are thinking should be the priorities. We also offer our own perspectives on this issue with a particular focus on what may help drive innovation in this area.

In order to safeguard athlete mental health and optimise competitive performance, continued recognition and understanding of athlete burnout is essential. We hope the present volume goes some way to doing so.

References

Gustafsson, H., DeFreese, J. D., & Madigan, D. J. (2017). Athlete burnout: Review and recommendations. *Current Opinion in Psychology*, *16*, 109–113.

Madigan, D. J., Olsson, L. F., Hill, A. P., & Curran, T. (2022). Athlete burnout symptoms are increasing: A cross-temporal meta-analysis of average levels from 1997 to 2019. *Journal of Sport and Exercise Psychology*, *44*, 153–168.

Nicholls, A. R., Madigan, D. J., Fairs, L. R., & Bailey, R. (2020). Mental health and psychological well-being among professional rugby league players from the UK. *BMJ Open Sport & Exercise Medicine*, 6, e000711.

Nixdorf, I., Frank, R., Hautzinger, M., & Beckmann, J. (2013). Prevalence of depressive symptoms and correlating variables among German elite athletes. *Journal of Clinical Sport Psychology*, 7, 313–326.

Purcell, R., Rice, S., Butterworth, M., & Clements, M. (2020). Rates and correlates of mental health symptoms in currently competing elite athletes from the Australian national high-performance sports system. *Sports Medicine*, *50*, 1683–1694.

Vella, S. A., Schweickle, M. J., Sutcliffe, J. T., & Swann, C. (2021). A systematic review and meta-synthesis of mental health position statements in sport: Scope, quality and future directions. *Psychology of Sport and Exercise*, *55*, 101946.

1 Recognising the Symptoms of Athlete Burnout

This chapter introduces athlete burnout. In doing so, our aim is to provide the means to understand what burnout is, how to recognise and measure burnout symptoms, and to examine the degree to which it is present in sport. This includes a discussion of recent evidence illustrating that athlete burnout levels are increasing, and have been doing so for the past two decades. But, first, we begin by providing some historical context before moving on to defining burnout and outlining details of how it is measured.

What Is Burnout?

Burnout has a relatively brief history in the psychological sciences. Work initially began in the early 1980s when two psychologists – Christina Maslach and Herbert Freudenberger – working independently, observed the development of a group of what seemed to be interrelated psychosocial complaints among those working in human services professions (Freudenberger, 1986; Maslach & Jackson, 1981). Following these observations, it was Maslach and her colleagues who forwarded the first formal definition of burnout. They defined burnout as an occupational psychosocial syndrome – meaning that it is experienced in relation to one's profession and is defined by its symptoms, of which there are three: (1) emotional exhaustion (feelings of being emotionally overextended and exhausted by one's work), (2) cynicism (a cynical and impersonal response towards people one works with), and (3) reduced efficacy (no longer feeling competent and successful at one's work; Maslach et al., 1986).

The introduction of a formal definition of burnout enabled a great deal of empirical research to be conducted. This work has supported the idea that chronic stress is integral to burnout development and has highlighted the many consequences of burnout for individuals (discussed further in Chapters 2 and 3). Perhaps the most important contemporary

DOI: 10.4324/9781003601098-1

advance has been that Maslach's definition has been adopted by the World Health Organization in their most recent revision of the International Classification of Diseases (Version 11; Harrison et al., 2021). While not strictly described as a disease itself, burnout is conceptualised as an occupational phenomenon that influences an individual's health status. And is therefore a factor implicated in an individual's need to engage with health services.

Since the early work amongst human services employees, burnout has been examined in a range of other occupations. This has included healthcare, education, and the workplace more broadly. Given the similarities between an athletic career and many other occupations (e.g., pressures, Arnold et al., 2017), and the many chances for stress exposure (including many training and competition stressors), sport has also been an area of interest for burnout researchers. Interestingly, in this regard, early on, Freudenberger (1975) noted that athletes may be a potential group to be heavily at risk of burnout. An important point to note, here, is that when examining burnout in different contexts it is necessary to account for the differences that exist between the activities an individual undertakes and their unique experiences in that particular context (e.g., competitive performance). For these reasons, when we talk about and examine burnout in athletes, we adopt an approach that contextualises the definition and symptoms of burnout to better reflect the situation and experiences of athletes. In the scientific literature, there have been two attempts to do so.

The first attempt to provide a definition of athlete burnout was provided by Eades (1990). Based on the original definition provided by Maslach and on interviews with athletes suffering from burnout, their definition differentiates (1) negative self-concept of athletic ability, (2) emotional and physical exhaustion, (3) psychological withdrawal from and devaluation of sport participation, (4) devaluation by coach and teammates, (5) congruent athlete-coach expectations, and (6) personal and athletic accomplishment (Eades, 1990, 1991).

Then, more recently, Raedeke and Smith (2001) provided a definition that matched, but contextualised to better reflect the nature of sport (e.g., physical demands), the three burnout symptoms proposed by Maslach. In doing so, they defined athlete burnout as (1) physical and emotional exhaustion, (2) sport devaluation, and (3) a reduced sense of athletic accomplishment (Raedeke & Smith, 2001). Physical and emotional exhaustion is characterised by the perceived depletion of emotional and physical resources resulting from training and competition. Sport devaluation is the development of a cynical attitude towards sport participation. Finally, a reduced sense of athletic accomplishment is characterised by a negative evaluation of one's sporting abilities and achievements.

How Is Burnout Measured?

In order to be able to understand and do something about burnout, we need robust ways to measure it. Luckily, there have been several notable developments in this regard. The first was the development of the Maslach Burnout Inventory (MBI; Maslach et al., 1986). This instrument was built off the back of the work and definition proposed by Maslach. The original MBI contains 22 items (questions), with 9 items capturing exhaustion, 5 items capturing cynicism, and 8 items capturing reduced efficacy. We have provided example items from this instrument in Table 1.1. Individuals respond to the items based on the frequency with which they have experienced them. Much work has supported the validity (it measures what we think it should) and reliability (it measures it consistently) of this instrument when measuring burnout in a range of work contexts. However, as these contexts have primarily been working populations and non-athlete populations, it is not recommended for use with athletes.

Mirroring the two formal definitions of athlete burnout, there are two instruments that have been used to measure burnout in athletes.

The first instrument developed exclusively for measuring athlete burnout was the Eades Athlete Burnout Inventory (EABI; Eades, 1990). This self-report instrument has 36 items. However, there is insufficient evidence for the validity of the EABI (e.g., Vealey et al., 1998). Moreover, studies have reported low internal consistency (items measuring things differently) for two of the EABI's subscales (e.g., Gould et al., 1996).

The second is Raedeke and Smith's (2001) Athlete Burnout Questionnaire (ABQ). This self-report instrument consists of 15 items, with 5 items reflecting physical and emotional exhaustion, 5 items reflecting sport devaluation, and 5 items reflecting a reduced sense of accomplishment. It asks athletes to reflect on the frequency with which they are experiencing these symptoms (*almost never* to *almost always*). We have provided sample items in Table 1.1. Unlike the EABI, the ABQ has been shown to be reliable and valid in a range of samples, sports, and across various age groups (Grugan et al., 2024). This has included evidence for its factor analytic structure, the internal consistency of scores, and its test-retest reliability (e.g., Raedeke & Smith, 2009). It has also been translated into many languages (e.g., French, Spanish, Chinese; Arce et al., 2012; Isoard-Gautheur et al., 2010; Liu et al., 2022). Importantly, as can be seen in Table 1.1, when comparing the MBI and ABQ, this realignment with work outside of sport in terms of adopting the same three symptom definition has also provided a strong theoretical and empirical basis for the study of burnout in athletes.

We have previously provided an expert statement on athlete burnout for the British Association of Sport and Exercise Sciences (Madigan

Table 1.1 Symptoms, example items, and response format for determining the frequency of burnout symptoms.

Symptom	*Original format (MBI)*	*Athlete format (ABQ)*	*Frequency*						
			Never			*Sometimes*			*Always*
Exhaustion	I feel exhausted at the end of a working day	I feel "wiped out" from my sport	0	1	2	3	4	5	6
Devaluation	I don't really care what happens to some patients	I don't care about my sport performance as I used to	0	1	2	3	4	5	6
Reduced accomplishment	I have not accomplished many worth-while things in this job	I am not achieving much in my sport	0	1	2	3	4	5	6

Note: MBI = Maslach Burnout Inventory. ABQ = Athlete Burnout Questionnaire. ABQ items are based on items with the highest factor loadings from analyses by Grugan et al. (2024). Adapted from Madigan et al. (2019). First published in The Sport and Exercise Scientist, Issue 61, Autumn 2019. Published by the British Association of Sport and Exercise Sciences – www.bases.org.uk

et al., 2019) with the aim of articulating how self-report measures could be used to monitor athlete burnout symptoms. Monitoring burnout is an important component of burnout prevention. To do so in athletes, we recommend using the ABQ. The items and response format in Table 1.1 give an example of how to do this. Higher scores of the ABQ are indicative of more frequent burnout symptoms.

Measuring burnout in this way may provide a useful snapshot of current burnout levels in athletes. Gaining knowledge of current burnout levels would be useful to identify those athletes most at risk. To make real use of this idea, however, continued completion and monitoring of burnout scores would enable sport scientists, psychologists, and coaches to get a handle on how athlete burnout symptoms are changing over time and to adjust training and support programmes accordingly. We see this as an essential first step to being able to protect athletes from burnout.

How Common Is Athlete Burnout?

Now that we know how to measure burnout, we can explore how often athletes experience burnout symptoms. In the broader psychological literature, this is perhaps the most well studied of all burnout questions.

Given the large volume of work, the research on burnout prevalence has been systematically collated, and this has been done across a range of contexts, including in healthcare, education, and other workplace settings.

Because they include so many studies, the reviews outside of sport give us a pretty good indication of how often individuals present with burnout symptomology. In this regard, estimates from these reviews suggest that burnout levels can range from 20% up to as high as 70%, depending on the context. For example, studies on nurses, students, and teachers provide estimates that are typically in the range of 20–30% (e.g., García-Carmona et al., 2019; Rosales-Ricardo et al., 2021; Woo et al., 2020). However, studies in physicians, in particular, suggest that rates are much higher; typically, 60–70% (Rotenstein et al., 2018). Despite the discrepancies, what is clear, then, is that burnout is a phenomenon that affects more than a handful of individuals, and in some professions may even be endemic.

There is, however, one issue with this work. As we have seen, burnout is typically measured based on the frequency with which individuals report symptoms (e.g., ranging from zero to six; Table 1.1). At which point on this frequency continuum should we be classifying an individual as "burnt-out"? Unfortunately, this question is difficult to answer. The complexities are perhaps best illustrated in the aforementioned review of burnout prevalence in physicians (Rotenstein et al., 2018). This review is notable for two reasons. First, one reason is the huge literature base that it summarises – 180 studies, which include over 100,000 physicians. Second, another reason is the variability in the cut-off used to denote burnout in the work that is summarised – 142 different approaches were taken to define an individual as "burnt-out" across these studies. The different approaches range from using specific scores on a single symptom to aggregating scores across symptoms, and many different ways in between. Consequently, the accuracy of prevalence estimates from this work should be used with a note of caution.

There are several ways to overcome the issues associated with cut-off scores. The most obvious would be to denote a universal cut-off score that all researchers could adopt. Work in this regard has provided some steer – but this is based on arbitrary cut offs usually from non-representative samples. The bigger question, however, is whether it makes sense to use cut-off values at all. This problem relates to the taxometric nature of burnout – that is, whether burnout is categorical (burnt out or not) or continuous (higher and lower levels of burnout symptoms). Most psychological phenomena are continuous (Haslam et al., 2020). In addition, we measure burnout in a manner consistent with the view that it is continuous, and it is also viewed theoretically as such.

In sport, we have proposed an option that aligns with the position of athlete burnout as continuous and that takes advantage of how burnout has been measured in sport. In this regard, we have sought to examine average burnout scores across studies (Madigan et al., 2022). To do so, following a systematic search of the literature, we collated all studies that had examined athlete burnout using the ABQ and had reported mean scores. We found 91 studies in total, which included over 21,000 athletes – making it the largest study on athlete burnout to date.

To examine the question of athlete burnout prevalence, we used a statistical technique known as meta-analysis. This technique involves collecting relevant data – in this case, means – then quantitatively summarising effects across the studies. To do so, meta-analysis takes into account between-study differences, and most importantly differing sample sizes across studies. This is important because larger sample sizes result in effect sizes (means) that are more accurate estimates of population effects (i.e., real-world effects). To do so, meta-analysis weights effects from individual studies based on their sample size – so that those studies with larger samples, and therefore more accurate estimates, are given more weight or strength in the overall analysis.

Our work was based on a variation of this technique known as cross-temporal meta-analysis. In addition to the weighting of effects, we also included the year in which the data were collected as a moderator (i.e., as a possible condition under which the effects may vary). Ultimately, this allowed us to examine whether average burnout scores varied as a function of the year in which the data were collected. By combining these analyses, we were able to examine mean level *change* of athlete burnout scores over the last two decades.

We found that average levels of two out of the three athlete burnout symptoms – sport devaluation and reduced athletic accomplishment – had significantly increased over the past twenty years. That is, athletes today are reporting, on average, more burnout symptoms than they were two decades ago. Importantly, too, we found little evidence that athlete burnout levels differ based on demographic factors – burnout does not seem to discriminate. To help visualise these trends, we have included illustrative graphs of these analyses in Figure 1.1.

What does this mean for sport? As we will see in Chapter 2, burnout negatively affects athletes in many ways, so having shown that burnout is increasing is indeed worrying. More importantly too, is that if this trend continues, many more athletes will be at risk of burnout and its consequences in the future.

There are several possible explanations for this finding. First, because sport is becoming increasingly professionalised, it is more competitive, and perhaps more intense than it ever has been. This includes the sheer number of other people that athletes have to compete against and also the volume of competitions that they need to compete in to progress, and this is apparent even at amateur levels of sport (e.g., Eime et al., 2016).

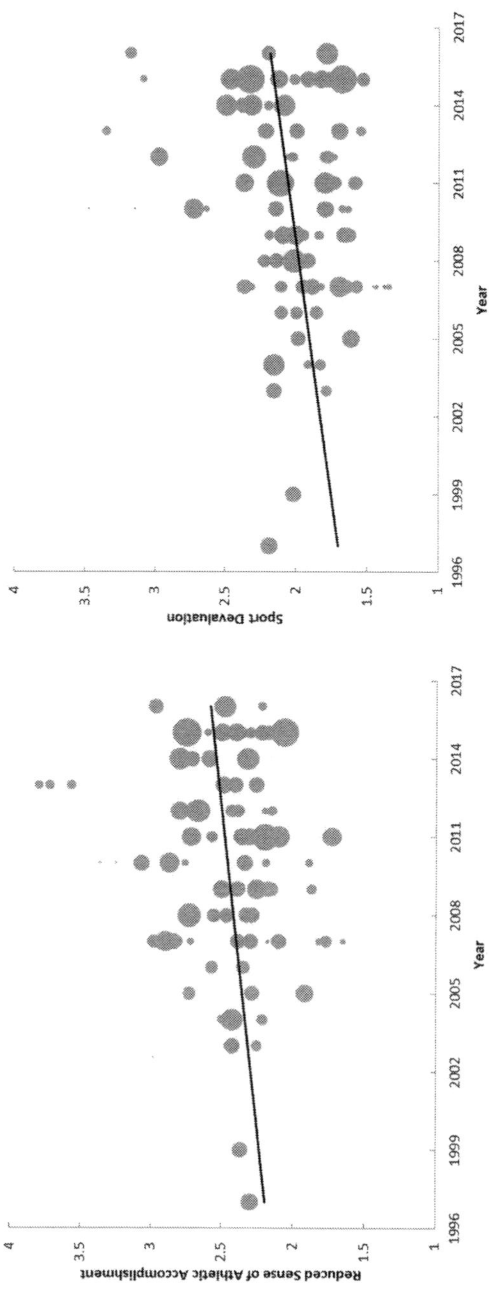

Figure 1.1 Changes in average athlete burnout symptoms over time.

Note: Circles represent individual study estimates (means). The size of each circle reflects its relative contribution to the overall estimate. Based on data available from Madigan et al. (2022).

Second, athletes are more likely to specialise in a sport, and to do so at an earlier age. So, they are not only more invested in their particular sport, but perhaps lack a breadth of experiences and learned coping skills that playing multiple sports would provide them (e.g., Normand et al., 2017). Finally, these changes appear to be accompanied by increasing external pressures, especially from parents and coaches who want their children and athletes to succeed (e.g., Gould, 2019). As we will see in Chapter 3, all of these factors have been implicated in burnout development.

Overall, then, it appears that athletes are thinking about their sport participation differently – they are perceiving fewer accomplishments, and they are less attached to their sport. The rest of this book seeks to provide further means to better understand and reverse this trend among athletes.

Conclusion

In this chapter, we have provided the foundations required to understand what burnout is and how we measure it. We consider athlete burnout to be a multidimensional syndrome of (1) physical and emotional exhaustion, (2) sport devaluation, and (3) a reduced sense of athletic accomplishment. The ABQ is the most appropriate instrument to measure these symptoms. The most recent evidence suggests that athlete burnout is becoming increasingly common, and should this pattern continue, more and more athletes will suffer from burnout and its consequences going forward.

References

Arce, C., De Francisco, C., Andrade, E., Seoane, G., & Raedeke, T. (2012). Adaptation of the Athlete Burnout Questionnaire in a Spanish sample of athletes. *The Spanish Journal of Psychology*, *15*, 1529–1536.

Arnold, R., Fletcher, D., & Daniels, K. (2017). Organisational stressors, coping, and outcomes in competitive sport. *Journal of Sports Sciences*, *35*, 694–703.

Eades, A. (1991) An investigation of burnout in intercollegiate athlete: The development of the Eades Athlete Burnout Inventory. *Paper presented at the North American Society for the Psychology of Sport and Physical Activity National Conference, Asilomar, CX.*

Eades, A. M. (1990). An Investigation of Burnout of Intercollegiate Athletes: The Development of the Eades Athlete Burnout Inventory. *Unpublished Master's Thesis, Berkley.*

Eime, R. M., Harvey, J. T., Charity, M. J., & Payne, W. R. (2016). Population levels of sport participation: Implications for sport policy. *BMC Public Health*, *16*(1), 8.

Freudenberger, H. J. (1986). The issues of staff burnout in therapeutic communities. *Journal of Psychoactive Drugs*, *18*, 247–251.

Freudenberger, H. J. (1975). Staff burn-out syndrome in alternative institutions. *Psychotherapy: Theory, Research and Practice*, *12*, 73e82.

García-Carmona, M., Marín, M. D., & Aguayo, R. (2019). Burnout syndrome in secondary school teachers: A systematic review and meta-analysis. *Social Psychology of Education*, *22*, 189–208.

Gould, D. (2019). The current youth sport landscape: Identifying critical research issues. *Kinesiology Review*, *8*, 150–161.

Gould, D., Tuffey, S., Udry, E., & Loehr, J. (1996). Burnout in competitive junior tennis players: I. A quantitative psychological assessment. *The Sport Psychologist*, *10*, 322–340.

Grugan, M. C., Olsson, L. F., Vaughan, R. S., Madigan, D. J., & Hill, A. P. (2024). Factorial validity and measurement invariance of the Athlete Burnout Questionnaire (ABQ). *Psychology of Sport and Exercise*, *73*, 102638.

Harrison, J. E., Weber, S., Jakob, R., & Chute, C. G. (2021). ICD-11: An international classification of diseases for the twenty-first century. *BMC Medical Informatics and Decision Making*, *21*, 1–10.

Haslam, N., McGrath, M. J., Viechtbauer, W., & Kuppens, P. (2020). Dimensions over categories: A meta-analysis of taxometric research. *Psychological Medicine*, *50*, 1418–1432.

Isoard-Gautheur, S., Oger, M., Guillet, E., & Martin-Krumm, C. (2010). Validation of a French version of the Athlete Burnout Questionnaire (ABQ). *European Journal of Psychological Assessment*, *26*, 203–211.

Liu, H., Wang, X., Wu, D. H., Zou, Y. D., Jiang, X. B., Gao, Z. Q., & Liu, J. D. (2022). Psychometric properties of the Chinese translated athlete burnout questionnaire: Evidence from Chinese collegiate athletes and elite athletes. *Frontiers in Psychology*, *13*, 823400.

Madigan, D. J., Gustafsson, H., Smith, A., Raedeke, T., & Hill, A. P. (2019). The BASES expert statement on burnout in sport. *The Sport and Exercise Scientist*, *61*, 6–7.

Madigan, D. J., Olsson, L. F., Hill, A. P., & Curran, T. (2022). Athlete burnout symptoms are increasing: A cross-temporal meta-analysis of average levels from 1997 to 2019. *Journal of Sport and Exercise Psychology*, *44*, 153–168.

Maslach, C., & Jackson, S. E. (1981). The measurement of experienced burnout. *Journal of Organizational Behavior*, *2*, 99–11.

Maslach, C., Jackson, S. E., Leiter, M. P., Schaufeli, W. B., & Schwab, R. L. (1986). *Maslach burnout inventory* (Vol. 21, pp. 3463–3464). *Palo Alto, CA: Consulting Psychologists Press*.

Normand, J. M., Wolfe, A., & Peak, K. (2017). A review of early sport specialization in relation to the development of a young athlete. *International Journal of Kinesiology and Sports Science*, *5*, 37–42.

Raedeke, T. D., & Smith, A. L. (2001). Development and preliminary validation of an athlete burnout measure. *Journal of Sport and Exercise Psychology*, *23*, 281–306.

Raedeke, T. D., & Smith, A. L. (2009). *The Athlete Burnout Questionnaire manual*. Morgantown, WV: West Virginia University.

Rosales-Ricardo, Y., Rizzo-Chunga, F., Mocha-Bonilla, J., & Ferreira, J. P. (2021). Prevalence of burnout syndrome in university students: A systematic review. *Salud Mental*, *44*, 91–102.

Rotenstein, L. S., Torre, M., Ramos, M. A., Rosales, R. C., Guille, C., Sen, S., & Mata, D. A. (2018). Prevalence of burnout among physicians: A systematic review. *JAMA*, *320*, 1131–1150.

Vealey, R. S., Armstrong, L., Comar, W., & Greenleaf, C. A. (1998). Influence of perceived coaching behaviors on burnout and competitive anxiety in female college athletes. *Journal of Applied Sport Psychology*, *10*, 297–318.

Woo, T., Ho, R., Tang, A., & Tam, W. (2020). Global prevalence of burnout symptoms among nurses: A systematic review and meta-analysis. *Journal of Psychiatric Research*, *123*, 9–20.

2 Reviewing the Consequences of Athlete Burnout

This chapter summarises recent research concerning the consequences of burnout. So as to provide a broad understanding of this issue, we start by reviewing studies that have been conducted outside of sport, before moving to those that have focused on athletes. Our aim is to provide readers with an idea of what can be expected when burnout symptoms arise, and thus why they should be avoided.

Consequences Outside of Sport

The early theoretical work of Maslach and colleagues outlined many possible consequences of burnout (e.g., Maslach et al., 2001). In the following section, we start by reviewing the large volume of literature that has developed over the past thirty years in relation to occupational burnout. In doing so, we focus our discussion on performance, attrition, health, and other miscellaneous outcomes.

Performance

The most prominent consequence of burnout that has been examined is reduced work performance. There are large economic implications of an ineffective workforce (e.g., Collins et al., 2005). More importantly, too, are the personal consequences of underperformance (e.g., losing one's job; Zimmerman & Darnold, 2009). Theory in this area posits several reasons why burnout will result in worse performance. Most notably, burnout may underpin an inability (a depletion of resources and a lack of energy that comprises exhaustion) and an unwillingness (disengagement as a result of the distance that cynicism creates between the individual and their work) to expend effort (Schaufeli & Taris, 2005). It may also lead to negative self-perceptions (from reduced efficacy) which result in a substantial loss of interest, and avoidance behaviours such as

DOI: 10.4324/9781003601098-2

absenteeism (arising from feelings of frustration, tension, and exhaustion). Performance suffers as a consequence.

As you may expect, much research has explored this idea. In this regard, a robust relationship between burnout and performance has indeed been found empirically. Several meta-analyses of research in this area serve to illustrate this point. One of the earliest such reviews included 16 longitudinal studies and showed workplace performance (such as customer satisfaction and supervisor appraisals) to deteriorate over time as a function of burnout symptomology (Taris, 2006). Similarly, Madigan and Curran (2021) showed in a very large sample of over 100,000 secondary and tertiary students (from high school, college, and university) that all symptoms of burnout significantly inhibit exam performance and are detrimental to the grades that students achieve both in individual classes and across whole educational programmes. Finally, the most recent account of this literature showed that effects translate across occupations but that some occupations are more affected than others (e.g., more likely in managerial than sales roles; Corbeanu et al., 2023).

Health

Much of the early theorising around burnout also focused on its implications for individuals' health (Shirom et al., 2005). There are several theoretical explanations in this regard. First, so as to cope with the experience of frequent burnout symptoms, individuals may be likely to engage in unhealthy behaviours. This may be while at work (e.g., consumption of junk food), at home (e.g., alcohol consumption), or both (e.g., lack of exercise/physical activity). Such behaviours are well-known risk factors for various physical ill-health consequences (e.g., cardiovascular disease). Second, burnout may modulate individuals' biophysiological responses to stress. For example, when presented with stressful situations, individuals experiencing frequent burnout symptoms are less able to respond biologically (e.g., blunted cortisol responses [hypocortisolism]; Danhof-Pont et al., 2011). Over time, these processes have implications for disease susceptibility, especially in context of autoimmune disorders and chronic pain. Finally, burnout may compromise individuals' immune systems (including, for example, immunoglobulin antibody secretion). It is therefore possible that individuals who experience frequent burnout symptoms are more susceptible to infectious disease and associated illness (see Bayes et al., 2021).

In terms of research supporting these positions, there are two recent reviews that are worth discussing. This includes a recent review summarising studies that have explored physical and psychological health (Salvagioni et al., 2017). This review included 61 studies that had adopted prospective designs (where individuals are followed over time and outcomes are reported in the future). This review found burnout to be a significant longitudinal predictor of mental health outcomes (e.g., insomnia), physical health outcomes (e.g., coronary heart disease), and occupational outcomes (e.g., job satisfaction). The most recent review focused specifically on teachers (Madigan et al., 2023). The findings showed that teacher burnout was consistently associated with somatic complaints (e.g., headaches), illnesses (e.g., gastroenteritis), voice disorders, and a range of stress biomarkers (e.g., cortisol).

Attrition

Another purported outcome of burnout with significant individual and economic consequences is dropout (e.g., Macdonald, 1999). It is thought that burnout experiences can result in individuals leaving their jobs entirely (Lee & Ashforth, 1996). In this regard, it is important to differentiate between the affective (emotional exhaustion and cynicism) and cognitive (reduced accomplishment) symptoms of burnout (Leiter, 1993). This is because the affective symptoms are associated with avoidant coping mechanisms that will likely lead to behavioural withdrawal, and, in extreme conditions, the desire to escape. Emotional exhaustion will cause individuals to feel drained and like they do not have the energy to spend another day at work (Schwab et al., 1986). Cynicism is also likely to increase interpersonal conflict with peers and other staff, and the reliance on withdrawal to minimise such conflict (Leiter & Maslach, 1988). While, on the other hand, reduced accomplishment is more likely to be tied to performance evaluations (actual and perceived). It will therefore likely be linked to reduced motivation and diminished self-esteem (Beer & Beer, 1992). All of which are factors with a purported role in whether someone will stay in or leave their job.

There is a growing body of evidence to support the idea that burnout fuels attrition. The best evidence comes from work examining individuals' intentions to quit (conscious plans to leave one's work). Findings from a systematic review of physicians suggest that the exhaustion dimension of burnout is particularly strongly related to intentions to leave (Williams et al., 2020). A more recent meta-analysis of teachers' experiences found that burnout was strongly associated with their intentions to quit, and that burnout was more important than other factors, such as how satisfied they were with their job (Madigan & Kim, 2021).

Other Consequences

There are many other outcomes relevant to burnout too. These include interpersonal consequences such as conflict, irritability, and worse communication (e.g., Van Droogenbroeck et al., 2014). Burnout will also negatively affect motivation – which may shift from autonomous to more controlled forms (Cazan, 2015). It is also possible that individuals' self-worth will be negatively affected (e.g., Rosse et al., 1991). Finally, it is even possible that burnout has implications for suicidal thoughts (Dyrbye et al., 2008).

Consequences in Sport

With research outside of sport as a backdrop, we now turn our attention to the consequences of burnout for athletes. There is reason to believe that athletes will also be at risk of many negative consequences. At their broadest, these consequences will likely be similar in some ways to work outside of sport, but importantly research has tried to account for the unique aspects of an athlete's career. In this regard, there have been a couple of theoretical attempts to understand what burnout might mean for athletes. We discuss these before moving onto empirical work.

The first attempt to provide a perspective on athlete burnout consequences was provided by Smith (1986; see Chapter 3 for full details of this model). Their cognitive-affective model outlines burnout as a process that is tied to stress. Smith's model posits that burnout development results in physiological and behavioural responses. These responses are defined as both physiological symptoms (e.g., fatigue and illness susceptibility) as well as mental health symptoms (e.g., anxiety and depression). Dropout is also outlined as a notable behavioural consequence.

The second, more recent, attempt to understand these relationships was provided by Gustafsson et al. (2011). In their model (see Chapter 3 for full details), that summarises and integrates dominant models of athlete burnout (including Smith's model), further health consequences such as impaired immune function and chronic inflammation are also outlined.

The most recent attempt to provide a framework to understand these issues focused on the health consequences of athlete burnout (Glandorf et al., 2025). The authors borrowed from allostatic load theory – which states that chronic stress exposure has a negative impact and increases disease risk via allostatic overload. Where allostatic overload is defined as a multisystem dysfunction in the hypothalamus-pituitary-adrenal (HPA) axis and immune, anabolic, and cardiovascular systems.

Collectively, these theoretical perspectives highlight a range of health and affective consequences. In considering athletes broadly, it is perhaps best to consider a combination of occupational and athlete burnout theories. Together, these views make it clear that burnout will have many negative implications for athletes.

Research in Sport

While many studies have examined athlete burnout, the majority have focused on the antecedents (i.e., predictors or factors that increase the risk) of athlete burnout. In this regard, there have been several recent summaries of this work, including meta-analyses of stress (Lin et al., 2022), motivation (Li et al., 2013), and perfectionism (Hill & Curran, 2016; see Chapter 3 for full discussion of possible antecedents). It was not until very recently, however, that concerted effort has been utilised to examine and summarise the consequences of burnout for athletes. This has included only a single review focused on possible health consequences so far (Glandorf et al., 2025). In the remainder of the chapter, we will examine the conclusions of this review, in addition to exploring some specific studies focused on outcomes of particular interest and relevance to athletes, with the aim of consolidating what we know in this area.

Health Consequences for Athletes

Glandorf et al. (2025) provided the first and, so far, only review of athlete burnout consequences. They sought to review and meta-analyse all research that had examined the health consequences of athlete burnout. In doing so, they reviewed 54 studies, which included nearly 14,000 athletes. Across these studies, athletes were on average 19.8 years old, just over a third of the sampled athletes were female, and a smaller percentage were elite athletes (competing at the highest levels in their sport; 15%).

The review evaluated 43 cross-sectional studies – studies where burnout and the consequences were measured at the same time. And 11 longitudinal studies – studies where burnout was measured initially, and the consequences were measured at some point in the future. Where there were enough studies on a particular consequence, the review provided a meta-analysis of effects (a quantitative summary of available data).

Following recommendations in the area (Krahn et al., 2021), the review grouped outcomes in relation to mental health and physical health. Mental health was further divided into those factors which would be considered negative – relating to mental illness or how mentally poor an individual is (Conway et al., 2019) – and positive – an individual's ability to value and engage with their life (Galderisi et al., 2015). This distinction was important as conceptually burnout would increase the former and decrease the latter – resulting in more mental illness and lower positive perceptions of their life. These groupings, including specific outcomes, are now discussed.

Negative Mental Health

The negative mental health outcomes that have been examined include depression, anxiety, addictive behaviour, insomnia, worry, mood disturbances, psychological distress, and body image dissatisfaction. We now provide an overview of the evidence for each of these outcomes, including the volume (how many studies have been conducted and what type of designs have been used) and findings.

Depression

Thirteen studies have examined the relationship between burnout and depression (a low mood and loss of pleasure and interest in activities over a prolonged period; Hammen, 2005). Eight studies were cross-sectional, and five were longitudinal. Across studies, burnout was positively correlated with depression and predicted increased depression over time. These relationships were supported by the meta-analysis.

Anxiety

Ten studies have examined the relationship between burnout and anxiety (characterised by tension, worry, and apprehension; Craske et al., 2011). All studies were cross-sectional. In the majority of studies, burnout was positively associated with anxiety. This was also the case in the meta-analysis.

Addictive Behaviour

Three studies have examined the relationship between burnout and addictive behaviour (e.g., exercise addiction; Berczik et al., 2012). All three studies were cross-sectional. The findings were mixed with some evidence for a positive relationship between burnout and exercise addiction, but no evidence for a relationship between burnout and alcohol dependence.

Insomnia

Two studies have examined the relationship between burnout and insomnia (a sleep disorder reflecting a persistent difficulty with getting to sleep or maintaining sleep; Morin & Benca, 2012). Both studies were longitudinal. Burnout was found to predict increases in insomnia over time in both studies.

Worry

Two studies have examined the relationship between burnout and worry (thinking about the future in a way that leaves you anxious or apprehensive; Freeston et al., 1994). Both studies were cross-sectional. In both studies, burnout was positively associated with worry.

Mood

Two studies have examined the relationship between burnout and mood (short-lived emotional states; Mayer & Gaschke, 1988). One study was cross-sectional, and the other was longitudinal. Burnout was positively associated with tension, anger and confusion. The findings were mixed, however, for fatigue in that there was support from one study but not the other.

Psychological Distress

Two studies have examined the relationship between burnout and psychological distress (set of painful mental and physical feelings and emotions; Ridner, 2004). One study was cross-sectional, and the other was longitudinal. For the most part, burnout was positively correlated with different types of distress (e.g., training distress).

Body Image Dissatisfaction

Two studies have examined the relationship between burnout and body image dissatisfaction (negative attitudes towards your physical appearance; Kostanski et al., 2004). Both studies were cross-sectional. The findings of one study showed that burnout was positively associated with body image dissatisfaction.

It appears that burnout has links with a range of negative mental health outcomes. These include specific disorders (e.g., insomnia) and also broad emotional and mood disturbances.

Positive Mental Health

The positive mental health outcomes examined include satisfaction, subjective vitality, and quality of life. We now outline the evidence for these outcomes too.

Satisfaction

Eleven studies have examined the relationship between burnout and satisfaction (contentment with various aspects of life; Pavot & Diener, 2008). Nine studies were cross-sectional, and two were longitudinal. Across studies, burnout was negatively associated with satisfaction. This was also found in the meta-analysis.

Subjective Vitality

Eight studies have examined the relationship between burnout and subjective vitality (the state of feeling alive and alert; Ryan & Frederick, 1997). Five studies were cross-sectional, and three were longitudinal. Burnout was negatively associated with subjective vitality. This was also the case in the meta-analysis.

Quality of Life

One cross-sectional study examined the relationship between burnout and quality of life (the level of enjoyment, comfort, and health; Felce & Perry, 1995). Burnout was negatively associated with quality of life.

In summarising the findings here, not only does athlete burnout increases the risk of mental health difficulties, it appears to reduce the potential for positive experiences or reflections in athletes' lives.

Physical Health

The physical health outcomes that were examined include biomarkers, physical and somatic symptoms, physiological indices, and injury. The evidence for each is now outlined.

Biomarkers

Eight studies have examined the relationship between burnout and biomarkers (hormones and proteins in the blood or saliva; Aronson & Ferner, 2017). Six were cross-sectional and two were longitudinal. Overall, the findings were mixed. Out of four studies to examine cortisol, only one showed a positive relationship with burnout. Evidence from one study suggested that burnout was related to Vitamin D status and iron levels. There were no relationships between burnout and secretory immunoglobulin A, testosterone, and C-reactive protein.

Physical and Somatic Symptoms

Five studies have examined the relationship between burnout and physical symptoms (physical signs or feelings that are out of the ordinary; De Haes et al., 1990). All studies were cross-sectional. Across studies, burnout was positively associated with physical symptoms. This was supported by the meta-analysis.

Physiological Indices

Four studies have examined the relationship between burnout and physiological indices (quantifiable physiological parameters). Three of the studies were cross-sectional, and one was longitudinal. Burnout was positively associated with blood volume per pulse and respiratory frequency. However, there were mixed findings for electroencephalogram (EEG) readings.

Injury

Two studies have examined the relationship between burnout and injury. Both studies were cross-sectional. In one study, burnout was positively correlated with injury and training days lost to injury but was not associated with these outcomes in the remaining study.

The findings in relation to physical health are perhaps the most complex. There are clear indications that burnout predisposes athletes to increased physical symptoms (such as headaches), but less clarity is found in relation to other biological and physiological outcomes. Unlike research outside of sport, there is much less evidence to support psychophysiological stress and immune function suppression. Perhaps this, though, given only a handful of studies, reflects the absence of evidence rather than evidence of absence.

Dropout from Sport

Much like in the occupational context, dropout is a significant problem in sport. The demands of sport can make for a difficult environment for many athletes. It appears that burnout can exacerbate these issues. For example, in interviews, "burnt-out" athletes have articulated being highly motivated, before developing burnout, and leaving their sport as a consequence (Gustafsson et al., 2008). There have been few empirical tests of this idea in sport. The most robust of these, however, was provided by Isoard-Gautheur et al. (2016). Their study examined burnout profiles (grouping athletes based on their symptoms) and whether group membership predicted playing status six years later. Their sample included over 450 athletes aged 14–18 years old who were enrolled in elite handball training centres in France. Once grouped, those athletes who had demonstrably higher burnout levels at the start of the study were significantly more likely to have stopped playing handball six years later. Although the study did not control for those athletes who would have grown too old to play for the associated cohort, burnout was still likely one of the factors leading to discontinuation in this sport. It appears, then, that burnout is a prominent factor that can put athletes at risk of dropout causing some to leave the sport that they enjoy and love.

Performance Impairment

Given the relevance of performance to athletes, and sport in general, it is unsurprising that researchers have considered the performance implications of burnout. This has included interview studies where participants have noted that they believe burnout to have negatively influenced their performance (e.g., Cresswell & Eklund, 2007; Gould et al., 1996). It has also included studies that have found a relationship between burnout and self-reported performance or performance satisfaction (e.g., Kvĕton et al., 2021). However, it was not until recently that empirical evidence for a relationship with objective performance outcomes was found. Using multiple samples of track and field athletes and swimmers, Olsson et al. (2025) examined the burnout-performance relationship both cross-sectionally and over time. Results showed that in at least two of the three samples burnout negatively predicted performance (how fast they ran or swam relative to their personal best). These effects were most notable for a reduced sense of accomplishment and sport devaluation, whereas emotional and physical exhaustion was unrelated to performance. Collectively, these findings suggest that certain athlete burnout symptoms may indeed have negative consequences for sport performance, and that this is the case when considering a single performance and peak performance over time.

Summarising the Consequences of Athlete Burnout

In Table 2.1, we have summarised the available evidence in terms of the consequences of athlete burnout in sport. We have also provided an indication of the level of evidence for each of the possible consequences. In doing so, much like others have done previously (e.g., Goodger et al., 2007), we have adopted an approach to providing an indication of the

Table 2.1 Summary of the possible consequences of athlete burnout and the evidence to support each relationship.

	# of studies/samples		*% of studies supporting relationship*	*Likely consequence?*
	Cross-sectional	*Longitudinal*		
Negative mental health				
Depression	9	5	100%	**Y**
Anxiety	10	–	100%	**Y**
Addictive behaviour	3	–	33%	?
Insomnia	–	2	100%	**Y**
Worry	2	–	100%	**Y**
Mood disturbances	1	1	50%	?
Psychological distress	1	1	50%	?
Body image dissatisfaction	2	–	50%	?
Positive mental health				
Satisfaction	9	2	82%	**Y**
Subjective vitality	5	3	88%	**Y**
Quality of life	1	–	100%	**Y**
Physical health				
Biomarkers	6	2	38%	?
Physical and somatic symptoms	5	–	100%	**Y**
Physiological indices	4	–	50%	?
Injury	2	–	50%	?
Dropout	–	1	100%	**Y**
Performance	2	1	100%	**Y**

Note: **Y** = likely consequence of burnout. ? = relationship is unclear at this time.

likelihood of each relationship, in addition to the volume of evidence available (cross-sectional and longitudinal studies).

As you can see the picture is one that is largely, if not wholly, negative. There are physical consequences (e.g., injury), mental consequences (e.g., anxiety), but also sport-specific consequences (e.g., reduced performance). The athlete's world is also viewed as less positive in general in terms of satisfaction, vigour, and quality.

These findings are broadly supportive of theory inside and outside of sport. Particularly in relation to some of the health and performance issues. Sport psychology theory, however, could be expanded further to focus more on possible sport outcomes while considering the health consequences of athlete burnout. This could include explicit reference to the aforementioned outcomes and could elaborate on the possible mechanisms underpinning these associations. A further integration of these facets would be beneficial to work in this area (see also Chapters 3 and 5 for more details).

Conclusion

There is a growing body of theory and research in sport regarding athlete burnout consequences, which we have reviewed in the present chapter. From this work, it is apparent that burnout has many negative consequences for athletes. These range from diminished physical and mental health to reduced performance. Protecting athletes from burnout will, therefore, also help prevent these deleterious consequences.

References

Aronson, J. K., & Ferner, R. E. (2017). Biomarkers—A general review. *Current Protocols in Pharmacology*, *76*, 9–23.

Bayes, A., Tavella, G., & Parker, G. (2021). The biology of burnout: Causes and consequences. *The World Journal of Biological Psychiatry*, *22*, 686–698.

Beer, J., & Beer, J. (1992). Burnout and stress, depression and self-esteem of teachers. *Psychological Reports*, *71*, 1331e1336.

Berczik, K., Szabó, A., Griffiths, M. D., Kurimay, T., Kun, B., Urbán, R., & Demetrovics, Z. (2012). Exercise addiction: Symptoms, diagnosis, epidemiology, and etiology. *Substance Use & Misuse*, *47*, 403–417.

Cazan, A. M. (2015). Learning motivation, engagement and burnout among university students. *Procedia-Social and Behavioral Sciences*, *187*, 413–417.

Collins, J. J., Baase, C. M., Sharda, C. E., Ozminkowski, R. J., Nicholson, S., Billotti, G. M., ... & Berger, M. L. (2005). The assessment of chronic health conditions on work performance, absence, and total economic impact for employers. *Journal of Occupational and Environmental Medicine*, *47*, 547–557.

Conway, C. C., Forbes, M. K., Forbush, K. T., Fried, E. I., Hallquist, M. N., Kotov, R., ... & Eaton, N. R. (2019). A hierarchical taxonomy of psychopathology can transform mental health research. *Perspectives on Psychological Science*, *14*, 419–436.

Corbeanu, A., Iliescu, D., Ion, A., & Spînu, R. (2023). The link between burnout and job performance: A meta-analysis. *European Journal of Work and Organizational Psychology*, *32*, 599–616.

Craske, M. G., Rauch, S. L., Ursano, R., Prenoveau, J., Pine, D. S., & Zinbarg, R. E. (2011). What is an anxiety disorder? *Focus*, *9*, 369–388.

Cresswell, S. L., & Eklund, R. C. (2007). Athlete burnout: A longitudinal qualitative study. *The Sport Psychologist*, *21*, 1–20.

Danhof-Pont, M. B., van Veen, T., & Zitman, F. G. (2011). Biomarkers in burnout: A systematic review. *Journal of Psychosomatic Research*, *70*, 505–524.

De Haes, J. C. J. M., Van Knippenberg, F. C. E., & Neijt, J. (1990). Measuring psychological and physical distress in cancer patients: Structure and application of the Rotterdam Symptom Checklist. *British Journal of Cancer*, *62*, 1034–1038.

Dyrbye, L. N., Thomas, M. R., Massie, F. S., Power, D. V., Eacker, A., Harper, W., ... & Shanafelt, T. D. (2008). Burnout and suicidal ideation among US medical students. *Annals of Internal Medicine*, *149*, 334–341.

Felce, D., & Perry, J. (1995). Quality of life: Its definition and measurement. *Research in Developmental Disabilities*, *16*, 51–74.

Freeston, M. H., Rhéaume, J., Letarte, H., Dugas, M. J., & Ladouceur, R. (1994). Why do people worry? *Personality and Individual Differences*, *17*, 791–802.

Galderisi, S., Heinz, A., Kastrup, M., Beezhold, J., & Sartorius, N. (2015). Toward a new definition of mental health. *World Psychiatry*, *14*, 231.

Glandorf, H. L., Madigan, D. J., Kavanagh, O., & Mallinson-Howard, S. H. (2025). Mental and physical health outcomes of burnout in athletes: A systematic review and meta-analysis. *International Review of Sport and Exercise Psychology*, *18*, 372–416.

Goodger, K., Gorely, T., Lavallee, D., & Harwood, C. (2007). Burnout in sport: A systematic review. *The Sport Psychologist*, *21*, 127–151.

Gould, D., Tuffey, S., Udry, E., & Loehr, J. (1996). Burnout in competitive junior tennis players: I. A quantitative psychological assessment. *The Sport Psychologist*, *10*, 322–340.

Gustafsson, H., Hassmén, P., Kenttä, G., & Johansson, M. (2008). A qualitative analysis of burnout in elite Swedish athletes. *Psychology of Sport and Exercise*, *9*, 800–816.

Gustafsson, H., Kenttä, G., & Hassmén, P. (2011). Athlete burnout: An integrated model and future research directions. *International Review of Sport and Exercise Psychology*, *4*, 3–24.

Hammen, C. (2005). Stress and depression. *Annual Review of Clinical Psychology*, *1*, 293–319.

Hill, A. P., & Curran, T. (2016). Multidimensional perfectionism and burnout: A meta-analysis. *Personality and Social Psychology Review*, *20*, 269–288.

Isoard-Gautheur, S., Guillet-Descas, E., & Gustafsson, H. (2016). Athlete burnout and the risk of dropout among young elite handball players. *The Sport Psychologist*, *30*, 123–130.

Květon, P., Jelínek, M., & Burešová, I. (2021). The role of perfectionism in predicting athlete burnout, training distress, and sports performance: A short-term and long-term longitudinal perspective. *Journal of Sports Sciences*, *39*, 1969–1979.

Kostanski, M., Fisher, A., & Gullone, E. (2004). Current conceptualisation of body image dissatisfaction: Have we got it wrong? *Journal of Child Psychology and Psychiatry*, *45*, 1317–1325.

Krahn, G. L., Robinson, A., Murray, A. J., Havercamp, S. M., Havercamp, S., Andridge, R., … & Witwer, A. (2021). It's time to reconsider how we define health: Perspective from disability and chronic condition. *Disability and Health Journal*, *14*, 101129.

Lee, R. T., & Ashforth, B. E. (1996). A meta-analytic examination of the correlates of the three dimensions of job burnout. *Journal of Applied Psychology*, *81*, 123–133.

Leiter, M. P. (1993). Burnout as a developmental process: Consideration of models. In W. B. Schaufeli, C. Maslach, & T. Marek (Eds.), *Series in applied psychology: Social issues and questions. Professional burnout: Recent developments in theory and research* (pp. 237–250). Washington, DC: Taylor & Francis.

Leiter, M. P., & Maslach, C. (1988). The impact of interpersonal environment on burnout and organizational commitment. *Journal of Organizational Behavior*, *9*, 297–308.

Li, C., Wang, C. J., & Kee, Y. H. (2013). Burnout and its relations with basic psychological needs and motivation among athletes: A systematic review and meta-analysis. *Psychology of Sport and Exercise*, *14*, 692–700.

Lin, C. H., Lu, F. J., Chen, T. W., & Hsu, Y. (2022). Relationship between athlete stress and burnout: A systematic review and meta-analysis. *International Journal of Sport and Exercise Psychology*, *20*, 1295–1315.

Macdonald, D. (1999). Teacher attrition: A review of literature. *Teaching and Teacher Education*, *15*, 835–848.

Madigan, D. J., & Curran, T. (2021). Does burnout affect academic achievement? A meta-analysis of over 100,000 students. *Educational Psychology Review*, *33*, 387–405.

Madigan, D. J., & Kim, L. E. (2021). Towards an understanding of teacher attrition: A meta-analysis of burnout, job satisfaction, and teachers' intentions to quit. *Teaching and Teacher Education*, *105*, 103425.

Madigan, D. J., Kim, L. E., Glandorf, H. L., & Kavanagh, O. (2023). Teacher burnout and physical health: A systematic review. *International Journal of Educational Research*, *119*, 102173.

Maslach, C., Schaufeli, W. B., & Leiter, M. P. (2001). Job burnout. *Annual Review of Psychology*, *52*, 397–422.

Mayer, J. D., & Gaschke, Y. N. (1988). The experience and meta-experience of mood. *Journal of Personality and Social Psychology*, *55*, 102.

Morin, C. M., & Benca, R. (2012). Chronic insomnia. *The Lancet*, *379*, 1129–1141.

Olsson, L. F., Glandorf, H. L., Black, J. F., Jeggo, R. E., Stanford, J. R., Drew, K. L., & Madigan, D. J. (2025). A multi-sample examination of the relationship between athlete burnout and sport performance. *Psychology of Sport and Exercise*, *76*, 102747.

Pavot, W., & Diener, E. (2008). The satisfaction with life scale and the emerging construct of life satisfaction. *The Journal of Positive Psychology*, *3*, 137–152.

Ridner, S. H. (2004). Psychological distress: Concept analysis. *Journal of Advanced Nursing*, *45*, 536–545.

Rosse, J. G., Boss, R. W., Johnson, A. E., & Crown, D. F. (1991). Conceptualizing the role of self-esteem in the burnout process. *Group & Organization Studies*, *16*, 428–451.

Ryan, R. M., & Frederick, C. (1997). On energy, personality, and health: Subjective vitality as a dynamic reflection of well-being. *Journal of Personality*, *65*, 529–565.

Salvagioni, D. A. J., Melanda, F. N., Mesas, A. E., González, A. D., Gabani, F. L., & Andrade, S. M. D. (2017). Physical, psychological and occupational consequences of job burnout: A systematic review of prospective studies. *PloS One*, *12*, e0185781.

Schaufeli, W. B., & Taris, T. W. (2005). The conceptualization and measurement of burnout: Common ground and worlds apart. *Work & Stress*, *19*, 256–262.

Schwab, R. L., Jackson, S. E., & Schuler, R. S. (1986). Educator burnout: Sources and consequences. *Educational Research Quarterly*, *10*, 14–30.

Shirom, A., Melamed, S., Toker, S., Berliner, S., & Shapira, I. (2005). Burnout and health review: Current knowledge and future research directions. *International Review of Industrial and Organizational Psychology*, *20*, 269–308.

Smith, R. (1986). Toward a cognitive-affective model of athletic burnout. *Journal of Sport Psychology*, *8*, 36–50.

Taris, T. W. (2006). Is there a relationship between burnout and objective performance? A critical review of 16 studies. *Work & Stress*, *20*, 316–334.

Van Droogenbroeck, F., Spruyt, B., & Vanroelen, C. (2014). Burnout among senior teachers: Investigating the role of workload and interpersonal relationships at work. *Teaching and Teacher Education*, *43*, 99–109.

Williams, E. S., Rathert, C., & Buttigieg, S. C. (2020). The personal and professional consequences of physician burnout: A systematic review of the literature. *Medical Care Research and Review*, *77*, 371–386.

Zimmerman, R. D., & Darnold, T. C. (2009). The impact of job performance on employee turnover intentions and the voluntary turnover process: A meta-analysis and path model. *Personnel Review*, *38*, 142–158.

3 Preventing Athlete Burnout

This chapter seeks to review existing models of burnout development with a view to providing the most appropriate prevention strategies for athlete burnout. To do so, we first provide an overview of both historical and more recent theoretical models of burnout development. This includes a discussion of models outside of sport, before moving to models specifically aimed at understanding athlete burnout. We then end by using this information to provide recommendations for the most effective prevention strategies for athlete burnout.

Theories of Burnout Development Outside of Sport

Many theoretical models have been forwarded to explain the development of burnout outside of sport. Each model focuses on different individual and organisational processes and characteristics that influence its development. The earliest and most popular models are based on stress and stress processes. These models include Maslach's original theoretical propositions along with models that have been built on stress theory (e.g., job demands resources). We will first discuss these models and their associated empirical evidence. We will then move on to models that are based on other factors (e.g., the social environment) and describe those models that have had the most impact on the field.

Stress Theory and the Job Demands-Resources Model

According to Maslach's original theorising, burnout symptoms are understood to arise primarily as the result of stress-related processes (Maslach et al., 2001). Consequently, to understand why burnout develops, this approach focuses on emotional and situational demands along with the resources available to cope with those demands. Maslach and Jackson (1981) therefore argue that exhaustion, cynicism, and reduced efficacy are the result of an imbalance between these demands

DOI: 10.4324/9781003601098-3

and resources. Furthermore, it is the demands (e.g., high workload) that have the most influence on exhaustion, whereas it is the resources (e.g., high social support) that can act as a protective factor in relation to cynicism and efficacy. From this perspective, burnout symptoms will develop in a particular order. If an individual experiences increasing demands, then this will overload their resources, leading, first, to exhaustion. So as to try to overcome this exhaustion, cynicism develops which is closely followed by reduced efficacy (Lee & Ashforth, 1996).

The Job Demands–Resources (JD-R) model provides a more contemporary stress-based framework to understand burnout development (Bakker & Demerouti, 2007). According to this model, individuals in any occupation experience job demands (aspects of the job that are psychologically costly) and job resources (aspects of the job that can be helpful), and they bring personal resources (characteristics of the person that can be helpful to the job) into the job. Much like with Maslach and colleague's theorising, burnout develops as a function of increasing demands and diminishing resources (e.g., Lesener et al., 2019; Nahrgang et al., 2011; Salvagioni et al., 2017). Resources may also act to buffer the effects of job demands on burnout.

Stress-based approaches to understanding burnout development have received a large amount of empirical support. For example, the JD-R model has been highlighted in being the most commonly used model for explaining the development of burnout in occupational health psychology (Lesener et al., 2019). Other systematic reviews and meta-analyses provide support for the components of stress models too (e.g., demands, resources, coping; Shin et al., 2014). It is clear, then, that an imbalance between demands and resources provides at least some of the basis for occupational burnout development.

Social Competence and Exchange Theories

The social context has also been posited to be key in terms of understanding burnout. In this regard, Harrison's (1983) social competency model was one of the earliest social-based explanations of burnout development. The model proposes that if an individual perceives that they can have a positive impact and are able to help the recipients of their work, they are at a lower risk of developing burnout (high social competency). However, if an individual perceives that they are not able to have a positive impact or are unable to help the recipients of their work (low social competency), they are at a greater risk of developing burnout. The social competency model also proposes that the social environment can influence an individual's vulnerability to burnout. That is, a supportive environment in which individuals receive regular informational feedback regarding their performance will leave an individual more likely to have perceptions of high social competency, and thus be at a lower risk of burnout.

Over a decade later, Schaufeli et al. (1996) offered a social exchange perspective to explain burnout development. In doing so, they borrowed the central tenants of Adams's (1965) Equity Theory and applied it to burnout. They proposed that burnout can develop following a lack of reciprocity in social relationships at work. That is, exhaustion develops following the draining of emotional resources because of a perceived imbalance between investments and outcomes in such relationships. Next, individuals are likely to invest further into the relationship but feel frustrated when their additional investments do not lead to their desired outcomes, resulting in psychologically distancing from the relationships (cynicism). Finally, given that the individual has withdrawn from the relationship, there are increased failures and thus a lack of perceived personal accomplishments.

Social models of burnout have received some empirical support. For example, Byrne (1994) found that those who lacked adequate peer support and informational performance feedback were more likely to experience higher levels of burnout (see also Navarro et al., 2010). In addition, there is longitudinal evidence that physicians who had a lack of reciprocity were more likely to experience higher levels of burnout at subsequent time-points (Bakker et al., 2000). Research has also found support for this approach in context of other relationships such as between colleagues, and the employee-organisation relationship (see Schaufeli, 2006). Although not as extensively tested, the available evidence supports some of the key aspects of a social approach to burnout development outside of sport.

Theories of Athlete Burnout Development

Many models have also been provided for understanding athlete burnout development specifically. These models similarly postulate athlete burnout development to be underpinned by a range of different factors. They have also included stress and psychosocial factors, but they have also focused on factors more heavily linked to sport participation including certain personality characteristics and motivation. These models provide alternative and sometimes complementary explanations of burnout. In this latter vein, elements of these models have also been grouped within an integrative model (Gustafsson et al., 2011). We will now review the most prominent of these models including a description of each one, an overview of the associated empirical support, and an evaluation of their utility.

The Cognitive-Affective Stress Model of Athlete Burnout

The earliest sport-specific model of burnout was proposed by Smith (1986). Akin to the original theorising of Maslach and colleagues, the model emphasises psychological stress and posits that burnout develops via a four-stage stress-based process. The first stage considers the demands that are placed on the athlete (e.g., high training loads, excessive expectations, and pressure from others). The second stage involves cognitive appraisal of these demands. All athletes will not interpret the demands similarly – some athletes will perceive the demands as more overwhelming than others and may even experience feelings of helplessness. The third stage concerns a physiological response (e.g., arousal). This response is only evident if the demand is perceived as overwhelming or threatening. Finally, the physiological response will lead to behavioural responses or coping strategies. When the appraisal of demands as overwhelming becomes continual, the athlete may respond by engaging in avoidant behaviours or withdrawal from the activity altogether (e.g., dropout). It is at this juncture that a key response to a chronic overload of demands is the development of burnout. Accordingly, athlete burnout is the result of chronic sport-related appraisals of psychological stress that are not effectively mitigated by coping efforts.

Out of all the models of athlete burnout development, Smith's (1986) model has been widely cited in the literature and has perhaps had the greatest influence on the field (see Gustafsson et al., 2014). In this regard, research has consistently found that the more athletes experience stress or utilise ineffective coping strategies (e.g., Madigan et al., 2020), the greater the risk of burnout. Notably, stress is one of the factors most strongly related to athlete burnout, as noted in a recent meta-analysis (e.g., Lin et al., 2022), and longitudinal studies have found that increases in psychological stress precede increases in athlete burnout (e.g., DeFreese & Smith, 2014). Collectively, these findings provide strong support for a stress-based interpretation of athlete burnout.

Self-Determination Theory

Ryan and Deci's (2002) self-determination theory (SDT) has also been used as a framework to understand athlete burnout development (Cresswell & Eklund, 2005, 2006a). This organismic theory argues that social environmental conditions are fundamental to motivated behaviour and health and are derived from fulfilment of three basic psychological needs (Ryan & Deci, 2017). These three basic needs are autonomy (an individual's opportunity for choice), competence (an individual's appraisal of their ability to be effective in their sport), and relatedness (an individual's level of connectedness with significant others). SDT assumes that characteristics of the social environment are critical to the level of need satisfaction or need thwarting that individuals experience (Ryan & Deci, 2000). When needs are satisfied, athletes develop intrinsic motives for participation – their participation is self-determined – and experience optimal health. When needs are thwarted, particularly within controlling environments (e.g., working with an authoritative coach), athletes develop less intrinsic motives for participation, and less optimal psychological and physical health. In this model, athlete burnout is a state of ill-being that results from psychological need thwarting over time and is characterised by less intrinsic motives for participation, and a lack of motivation altogether (Lonsdale et al., 2009).

There is growing empirical research examining SDT and athlete burnout, this is both within individual studies and when studies have been summarised via meta-analysis (Li et al., 2013). In accordance with the theory, need thwarting is positively associated and need satisfaction is negatively associated with athlete burnout. In addition, athlete burnout is positively associated with amotivation and negatively associated with intrinsic motivation. Coach created climates that focus on autonomy are also negatively associated with athlete burnout, while those based on controlling coaching practices are positively associated with athlete burnout (Bartholomew et al., 2011). Over time, too, motivation and athlete burnout show similar patterns of change (e.g., Cresswell & Eklund, 2005). Thus, it is possible that chronically frustrated or unfulfilled psychological needs, as a result of the social environment, will lead to athlete burnout and that altered motivational regulation is an integral part of this process.

Perfectionism-Athlete Burnout Theory

Another major theory that has been used to understand athlete burnout development relates to the construct of perfectionism. Trait perfectionism is an achievement-related characteristic that reflects excessively high personal standards which are accompanied by overly critical evaluations of performance (Frost et al., 1990). Because many models and measures of trait perfectionism exist, a higher-order framework has been developed that differentiates two broad dimensions labelled perfectionistic strivings (PS) and perfectionistic concerns (PC; Stoeber & Otto, 2006). PS is characterised by aspects of perfectionism associated with striving for perfection and the setting of high personal standards. In contrast, PC is characterised by concerns over making mistakes, negative reactions to imperfection, socially prescribed pressures, and discrepancies between one's expectations and performance (Gotwals et al., 2012). From a theoretical perspective, perfectionism may lead to athlete burnout because of a tendency to create, maintain, magnify, and even anticipate stressful events. This is because highly perfectionistic athletes pursue goals that are irrational and unrealistic, engage in ineffective coping strategies, experience self-defeating thoughts, and worry about the future (Hewitt & Flett, 2002). As such, perfectionism may engender stress in athletes and leave them vulnerable to burnout.

Recently, the concept of perfectionism has been extended to the social environment. That is, the social environment and associated goal structures and cues can themselves be perfectionistic – and therefore athletes can find themselves in more or less perfectionistic environments. This idea is captured within the concept of the *perfectionistic climate* (Hill & Grugan, 2020). The perfectionistic climate comprises five distinct and interrelated components representing expectations (key social agents hold and demand unrealistic performance expectations of others), criticism (key social agents engage in harsh criticism whenever the performance of others is not perfect), control (key social agents employ externally controlling strategies that place pressure on others to perform perfectly), conditional regard (key social agents employ internally controlling strategies that place pressure on others to perform perfectly), and anxiousness (key social agents are extremely worried and vigilant about mistakes and the consequences of others not performing perfectly; Grugan et al., 2021). Given that the coach is the most important social agent influencing athletes' experiences – it is the training and competing environment that is most relevant when considering the perfectionistic climate for athletes. There are two main mechanisms through which the perfectionistic climate could lead to athlete burnout. The first is via increased trait perfectionism for the athlete – that is, pressures from the climate to be perfect are internalised and manifest in increased levels of PS and PC. The second is a more direct link with stress – perfectionistic climates are stressful. It is through these mechanisms that perfectionistic aspects of the social environment may lead to athlete burnout. We have summarised these pathways in Figure 3.1.

There is much empirical support for the links between perfectionism and athlete burnout. This has included meta-analytic reviews of cross-sectional work (Hill & Curran, 2016). But also, a growing number of longitudinal studies (e.g., Madigan et al., 2015; 2016). In each instance, it is PC that appear to provide the stronger impetus for athlete burnout. Work on the perfectionistic climate is in its infancy. However, the work that does exist points to support for our theoretical propositions (e.g., Olsson et al., 2022). For example, there is a large body of evidence showing that aspects of the climate (such as expectations and criticism) are related to increased trait perfectionism (Curran & Hill, 2022). Regarding the more direct pathway, in particular, there is also evidence of strong links between the climate and stress (Meng et al., 2024). It is

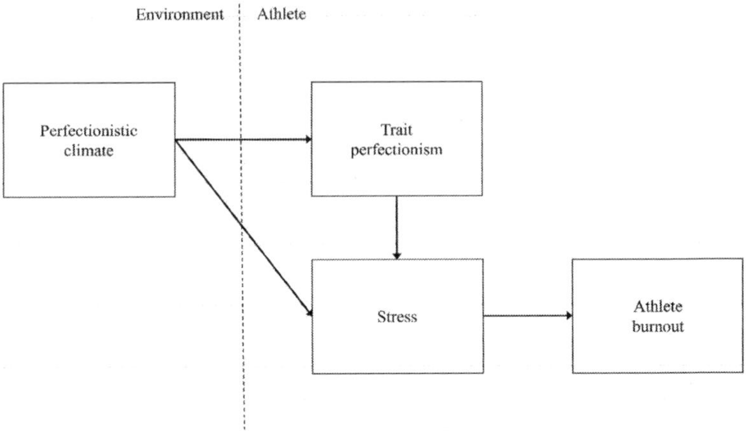

Figure 3.1 Overview of perfectionism-athlete burnout theory.

therefore possible that perfectionism – both as a trait and feature of the environment – underpins athlete burnout development.

The Integrated Model of Athlete Burnout

The final model of athlete burnout development was conceived by Gustafsson et al. (2011). Instead of providing an alternative explanation, the model attempts to provide a more holistic perspective by integrating the aforementioned models, or their most relevant attributes. The integrated model therefore provides key antecedents that include personality, coping, and the environment. In doing so, all these aspects are seen to act on both the early signs of burnout (e.g., mood disturbance, diminished motivation) and burnout itself.

The Integrated Model also includes other models of burnout development that have less empirical support. For example, Silva (1990) proposed a model that suggested that training stress was responsible for burnout. In this model, training stress is primarily concerned with training demands and posits that training stress can be positive or negative. On the one hand, adaptation to training stress will lead to enhanced performance. On the other hand, maladaptation to training stress can result in the experience of burnout and eventual withdrawal from sport. An alternative model from Coakley (1992) suggests that burnout develops due to a lack of control and restrictions to one's own identity. Specifically, Coakley suggests that burnout is a product of the structure of competitive sport and its capacity to exert control over an athlete and their life. Finally, Raedeke (1997) offered a commitment-based model that considers the desire and willingness to continue sport participation can be based on enjoyment or entrapment. Based on this idea, three possible profiles were proposed: low commitment (a lack of desire to participate), entrapment-based commitment (a need to participate), and attraction-based commitment (a desire to participate, based largely on enjoyment). The model suggests that entrapment-based commitment will render athletes more vulnerable to negative consequences. Thus, it is likely that athletes will be more likely to experience burnout if they are participating in their sport for entrapment-based reasons. There is a need to be cautious considering the sparse empirical evidence supporting these models. In addition, there are several other issues including the conflation of constructs (e.g., burnout and overtraining, burnout and dropout) and overlap with other models (commitment and SDT) that prohibit the recommended use of such models themselves in sport.

These limitations aside, Gustafsson et al.'s (2011) integrated model is widely cited within the athlete burnout literature. The research above examining individual components of the framework (e.g., environment, perfectionism) provides clear support for these particular pathways. However, empirical examination of the integrated nature of its components remains scarce (Eklund & DeFreese, 2020). Consequently, currently, the model is best-suited to direct future work examining the most important predictors of athlete burnout, and how they may interact with one another.

Athlete Burnout Prevention

Now that we have outlined the approaches to understanding burnout development both inside and outside of sport, there is an opportunity to use this knowledge to inform the advancement of prevention strategies for athlete burnout. The remainder of the present chapter, therefore, aims to provide strategies for creating conditions conducive to athlete burnout prevention. In this regard, we focus particularly on primary prevention (i.e., intervening before burnout develops) because it has the potential to significantly reduce the burden on healthcare systems, sports organisations, and athletes themselves (however, see also Chapter 4 for a review of interventions). In doing so, we focus on three approaches: coping effectively with stress, changing coaching behaviour, and increasing perfectionism literacy. It is recommended that these are utilised with the support of a suitably qualified practitioner (e.g., sport and exercise psychologist). Next, then, we present our thoughts regarding each of these approaches.

Coping Effectively with Stress

Stress is the most frequently cited theoretical precursor to burnout development. This is true of models outside of sport, and in the context of athletes as well. According to these theories, a particularly important resource in mitigating the development of chronic stress is coping (Demerouti et al., 2001). Coping refers to the cognitive and behavioural effort that an individual makes in order to manage internal and external sources of stress (Lazarus & Folkman, 1984). For athletes, coping is important for managing both stresses related to training and non-training-related stress (Raedeke & Smith, 2004). Research suggests that athletes use a wide range of coping strategies in order to try to reduce stress and can be adept at dealing with the challenges and threats they encounter (Nicholls & Polman, 2007). In sport, when coping is effective it can ensure optimal performance, maintain motivation, and safeguard wellbeing (Crocker et al., 2015). It has also been shown to be key in protecting athletes from burnout risk (e.g., Madigan et al., 2020).

How then may we help athletes cope with stress? In our opinion, it seems particularly important to adopt two particular approaches. First, is to provide athletes with a wide range of coping strategies to choose from. And second is to highlight which coping strategies are likely to be most effective or ineffective. There is some work in sport looking at what has been termed Coping Effectiveness Training which seeks to address these two aims (see Reeves et al., 2011). This training has two main parts that mirror these aims, which we now discuss below.

First, athletes can be taught a range of likely effective cognitive, behavioural, and emotional strategies. This can include problem-focused strategies aimed at removing sources of stress such as planning (making action plans), active coping (trying different things), and suppression of competing activities (stopping other things to focus on sport). In regards to burnout, problem-focused coping may help athletes to develop a sense of purpose and mobilise inner resources that are engaged towards sport-related activities and goal engagement (Nicholls et al., 2016). In addition, because resources are appropriately allocated to dealing with tasks and situations, coping resources are not unnecessarily depleted over time. As such, athletes still have an array of resources to deal with the varying situational demands that arise in competitive sport.

Second, athletes can be educated with regards to which coping strategies are likely ineffective. This can include avoidant coping strategies aimed at evading sources of stress such as denial (pretending things are not happening) and behavioural disengagement (giving up one's goals). In regards to burnout, the effort required to reorient away from dealing with demands and negative emotions can be physically and emotionally taxing and lead to chronic stress.

In order to make the most of such training, any tasks and education should be contextualised to the specific sport and/or event (e.g., training, competition; Nicholls, 2007). Developing athlete coping skills will be important to reduce chronic appraisals of stress and therefore athlete burnout development. Importantly, this should be considered against a backdrop of other recovery guidelines and recommendations to maximise physical recovery and thus reduce physical stress simultaneously (e.g., Kellmann et al., 2018).

Changing Coaching Practices

Altering the social environment is perhaps one of the most effective ways to protect athletes from burnout. This is because the coaching environment is controllable – that is, coaches can be taught to coach in certain ways that lead to more positive outcomes, including lower athlete burnout risk. In this regard, SDT has been used successfully as the means to create interventions to enhance autonomy supportive environments, and subsequent burnout protection for athletes. There is a large body of work outside of sport supporting these ideas. There is also some evidence in sport. Most notably, for example, Langan et al. (2015) based their athlete burnout intervention on SDT. To do so, they trained coaches to adopt strategies designed to increase their provision of need support and reduce their use of a controlling interpersonal style (e.g., Reeve, 2009). Following six training sessions in the experimental group, no changes in burnout were found, but increases in burnout were found in the control group. This finding tentatively suggests that the intervention may have attenuated any potential increases in burnout over the study period.

How may we help coaches create autonomy supportive environments? SDT provides the theoretical background to do so (e.g., Mageau & Vallerand, 2003). This includes highlighting what may be most important in context of an athlete's three basic psychological needs (see also Ahmadi et al., 2023).

In terms of autonomy, the goal is to create an environment where athletes feel volition, personal ownership, and endorse their sport participation. This can include allowing for athlete input, and providing choice, and allowing time for self-paced learning. In terms of competence, the goal is to create an environment where athletes feel capable of achieving their performance goals. This can include providing specific feedback and praising effort. In terms of relatedness, the goal is to create an environment where athletes feel accepted, understood, and worthy of attention from others including their teammates and coaches. This can include being patient and asking athletes about their progress. On the other side, coaches should avoid behaviours that are controlling.

Examples of such behaviours include being pressuring with language and deadlines, being critical of losing, especially publicly and in context of normative comparisons, ignoring athletes, and raising one's voice.

Adopting such a coaching strategy will mean that athletes have the greatest chance of being motivated for self-determined reasons (e.g., because they want to). This approach will also likely reduce the demands on an athlete and therefore mitigate some sources of stress. Ultimately, this approach should help produce an environment conducive to athlete burnout prevention.

Increasing Perfectionism Literacy

Our final suggestion for burnout prevention relates to perfectionism. In this regard, we believe that increasing perfectionism literacy of athletes and coaches will be beneficial. The concept of perfectionism literacy was recently introduced to the broader mental health literacy research (Etherson et al., 2025). It is defined as (a) the ability to recognise perfectionism, (b) knowledge of how to seek information regarding perfectionism, (c) knowledge of risk factors and causes of perfectionism, (d) knowledge of self-treatment and professional treatments available for perfectionism, and (e) attitudes that endorse recognition and help-seeking behaviour for perfectionism. Perfectionism literacy is related to greater help-seeking and reduced stigma of mental health problems. Given the strong links between perfectionism and burnout, it is therefore likely to help protect athletes from the stress that will ultimately lead to burnout. There is initial evidence that perfectionism literacy can be increased via informational/educational intervention (Etherson et al., 2025). There is a range of freely available resources with the intention of enhancing knowledge and beliefs about perfectionism. These include informational videos (Hill et al., 2021), fact sheets (Hill et al., 2018), and associated worksheets (Hill et al., 2019). Coaches and athletes may benefit from reviewing these documents to raise awareness of perfectionism and to help protect against athlete burnout development.

Conclusion

This chapter has provided an overview of the different ways researchers have explained the development of burnout, both outside and inside of sport. In doing so, we have outlined varying degrees of empirical support for each theoretical lens and their associated criticisms. In the applied context, it remains important that those working with athletes are using the research as a basis to actively seek to prevent the onset of burnout. Doing so is a way to better equip athletes with the tools to navigate the often-pressuring environment of sport as well as to promote more positive experiences for athletes.

References

Adams, J. S. (1965). Inequity in social exchange. *Advances in Experimental Social Psychology*, 2, 267–299.

Ahmadi, A., Noetel, M., Parker, P., Ryan, R. M., Ntoumanis, N., Reeve, J., … & Lonsdale, C. (2023). A classification system for teachers' motivational behaviors recommended in self-determination theory interventions. *Journal of Educational Psychology*, *115*, 1158.

Bakker, A. B., & Demerouti, E. (2007). The job demands-resources model: State of the art. *Journal of Managerial Psychology*, *22*, 309–328.

Bakker, A. B., Schaufeli, W. B., Sixma, H. J., Bosveld, W., & Van Dierendonck, D. (2000). Patient demands, lack of reciprocity, and burnout: A five-year longitudinal study among general practitioners. *Journal of Organizational Behavior*, *21*, 425–441.

Bartholomew, K. J., Ntoumanis, N., Ryan, R. M., Bosch, J. A., & Thøgersen-Ntoumani, C. (2011). Self-determination theory and diminished functioning: The role of interpersonal control and psychological need thwarting. *Personality and Social Psychology Bulletin*, *37*, 1459–1473.

Byrne, B. M. (1994). Burnout: Testing for the validity, replication, and invariance of causal structure across elementary, intermediate, and secondary teachers. *American Educational Research Journal*, *31*, 645–673.

Coakley, J. (1992). Burnout among adolescent athletes: A personal failure or social problem? *Sociology of Sport Journal*, *9*, 271–285.

Cresswell, S. L., & Eklund, R. C. (2005). Motivation and burnout in professional rugby players. *Research Quarterly for Exercise and Sport*, *76*, 370–376.

Cresswell, S. L., & Eklund, R. C. (2006a). Changes in athlete burnout over a thirty-week "rugby year". *Journal of Science and Medicine in Sport*, *9*, 125–134.

Crocker, P. R. E., Tamminen, K. A., & Gaudreau, P. (2015). Coping in sport. In S. D. Mellalieu & S. Hanton (Eds.), *Contemporary advances in sport psychology: A review* (pp. 28–67). New York, NY: Routledge/Taylor & Francis Group.

Curran, T., & Hill, A. P. (2022). Young people's perceptions of their parents' expectations and criticism are increasing over time: Implications for perfectionism. *Psychological Bulletin*, *148*, 107.

DeFreese, J. D., & Smith, A. L. (2014). Athlete social support, negative social interactions, and psychological health across a competitive sport season. *Journal of Sport and Exercise Psychology*, *36*, 619–630.

Demerouti, E., Bakker, A. B., Nachreiner, F., & Schaufeli, W. B. (2001). The job demands-resources model of burnout. *Journal of Applied Psychology*, *86*, 499.

Eklund, R. C., & DeFreese, J. D. (2020). Athlete burnout. In G. Tenenbaum, & Eklund, R. C. (Eds.), *Handbook of sport psychology* (pp. 1220–1240). New York: John Wiley & Sons.

Etherson, M. E., Hill, A. P., Grugan, M. C., Madigan, D. J., & Smith, M. M. (2025). Development and validation of the perfectionism literacy questionnaire. *Journal of Psychoeducational Assessment*, *43*, 273–295.

Frost, R. O., Marten, P., Lahart, C., & Rosenblate, R. (1990). The dimensions of perfectionism. *Cognitive Therapy and Research*, *14*, 449–468.

Gotwals, J. K., Stoeber, J., Dunn, J. G., & Stoll, O. (2012). Are perfectionistic strivings in sport adaptive? A systematic review of confirmatory, contradictory, and mixed evidence. *Canadian Psychology*, *53*, 263.

Grugan, M. C., Hill, A. P., Mallinson-Howard, S. H., Donachie, T. C., Olsson, L. F., Madigan, D. J., & Vaughan, R. S. (2021). Development and initial validation of the Perfectionistic Climate Questionnaire-Sport (PCQ-S). *Psychology of Sport and Exercise*, *56*, 101997.

Gustafsson, H., Hancock, D. J., & Côté, J. (2014). Describing citation structures in sport burnout literature: A citation network analysis. *Psychology of Sport and Exercise*, *15*, 620–626.

Gustafsson, H., Kenttä, G., & Hassmén, P. (2011). Athlete burnout: An integrated model and future research directions. *International Review of Sport and Exercise Psychology*, *4*, 3–24.

Harrison, W. D. (1983). A social competence model of burnout. In B. A. Farber (Ed.), *Stress and burnout in the human services professions* (pp. 29–39). New York: Pergamon Press.

Hewitt, P. L., & Flett, G. L. (2002). Perfectionism and stress in psychopathology. In G. L. Flett, & P. L. Hewitt (Eds.), *Perfectionism: Theory, research, and treatment* (pp. 255–284). Washington, DC: APA Press

Hill, A. P., & Curran, T. (2016). Multidimensional perfectionism and burnout: A meta-analysis. *Personality and Social Psychology Review*, *20*, 269–28.

Hill, A. P., & Grugan, M. (2020). Introducing perfectionistic climate. *Perspectives on Early Childhood Psychology and Education*, *4*, 263–276.

Hill, A. P., Madigan, D. J., Mallinson-Howard, S. H., & Smith, M. M. (2018) Perfectionism fact sheet. York St John University. Retrieved from: https://ray.yorksj.ac.uk/id/eprint/2966/

Hill, A. P., Madigan, D. J., Mallinson-Howard, S. H., & Smith, M. M. (2019) Perfectionism worksheets. York St John University. Retrieved from: https://ray.yorksj.ac.uk/id/eprint/4788/

Hill, A. P., Madigan, D. J., Mallinson-Howard, S. H., & Smith, M. M. (2021). Perfectionism animation (English). York St John University. Retrieved from: https://doi.org/10.25421/yorksj.16628734.v2

Kellmann, M., Bertollo, M., Bosquet, L., Brink, M., Coutts, A. J., Duffield, R., ... & Beckmann, J. (2018). Recovery and performance in sport: Consensus statement. *International Journal of Sports Physiology and Performance*, *13*, 240–245.

Langan, E., Toner, J., Blake, C., & Lonsdale, C. (2015). Testing the effects of a self-determination theory-based intervention with youth Gaelic football coaches on athlete motivation and burnout. *The Sport Psychologist*, *29*, 293–301.

Lazarus, R. S., & Folkman, S. (1984). *Stress, appraisal, and coping*. New York: Springer.

Lee, R. T., & Ashforth, B. E. (1996). A meta-analytic examination of the correlates of the three dimensions of job burnout. *Journal of Applied Psychology*, *81*, 123.

Lesener, T., Gusy, B., & Wolter, C. (2019). The job demands-resources model: A meta-analytic review of longitudinal studies. *Work & Stress*, *33*, 76–103.

Li, C., Wang, C. J., & Kee, Y. H. (2013). Burnout and its relations with basic psychological needs and motivation among athletes: A systematic review and meta-analysis. *Psychology of Sport and Exercise*, *14*, 692–700.

Lin, C. H., Lu, F. J., Chen, T. W., & Hsu, Y. (2022). Relationship between athlete stress and burnout: A systematic review and meta-analysis. *International Journal of Sport and Exercise Psychology*, *20*, 1295–1315.

Lonsdale, C., Hodge, K., & Rose, E. (2009). Athlete burnout in elite sport: A self-determination perspective. *Journal of Sports Sciences*, *27*, 785–795.

Madigan, D. J., Rumbold, J. L., Gerber, M., & Nicholls, A. R. (2020). Coping tendencies and changes in athlete burnout over time. *Psychology of Sport and Exercise*, *48*, 101666.

Madigan, D. J., Stoeber, J., & Passfield, L. (2015). Perfectionism and burnout in junior athletes: A three-month longitudinal study. *Journal of Sport and Exercise Psychology*, *37*, 305–315.

Madigan, D. J., Stoeber, J., & Passfield, L. (2016). Perfectionism and changes in athlete burnout over three months: Interactive effects of personal standards and evaluative concerns perfectionism. *Psychology of Sport and Exercise*, *26*, 32–39.

Mageau, G. A., & Vallerand, R. J. (2003). The coach-athlete relationship: A motivational model. *Journal of Sports Sciences*, *21*, 883–904.

Maslach, C., & Jackson, S. E. (1981). The measurement of experienced burnout. *Journal of Organizational Behavior*, *2*, 99–113.

Maslach, C., Schaufeli, W. B., & Leiter, M. P. (2001). Job burnout. *Annual Review of Psychology*, *52*, 397–422.

Meng, M., Su, R. H., Kogiso, K., Zheng, R. R., Chen, L., Wei, W., … & Hsu, M. C. (2024). How the perfectionistic climate of a sports team predicts the athletic performance of elite athletes: a case study of the CUBAL women's basketball team. *Frontiers in Psychology*, *15*, 1415196.

Nahrgang, J. D., Morgeson, F. P., & Hofmann, D. A. (2011). Safety at work: A meta-analytic investigation of the link between job demands, job resources, burnout, engagement, and safety outcomes. *Journal of Applied Psychology*, *96*, 71.

Navarro, M. L. A., Mas, M. B., & Jiménez, A. M. L. (2010). Working conditions, burnout and stress symptoms in university professors: Validating a structural model of the mediating effect of perceived personal competence. *The Spanish Journal of Psychology*, *13*, 284–296.

Nicholls, A. R. (2007). Can an athlete be taught to cope more effectively? The experiences of an international-level adolescent golfer during a training program for coping. *Perceptual and Motor Skills*, *104*, 494–500.

Nicholls, A. R., Levy, A. R., Carson, F., Thompson, M. A., & Perry, J. L. (2016). The applicability of self-regulation theories in sport: Goal adjustment capacities, stress appraisals, coping, and well-being among athletes. *Psychology of Sport and Exercise*, *27*, 47–55.

Nicholls, A. R., & Polman, R. C. (2007). Coping in sport: A systematic review. *Journal of Sports Sciences*, *25*, 11–31.

Olsson, L. F., Madigan, D. J., Hill, A. P., & Grugan, M. C. (2022). Do athlete and coach performance perfectionism predict athlete burnout? *European Journal of Sport Science*, *22*, 1073–1084.

Raedeke, T. D. (1997). Is athlete burnout more than just stress? A sport commitment perspective. *Journal of Sport and Exercise Psychology, 19*, 396–417.

Raedeke, T. D., & Smith, A. L. (2004). Coping resources and athlete burnout: An examination of stress mediated and moderation hypotheses. *Journal of Sport and Exercise Psychology, 26*, 525–541.

Reeve, J. (2009). Why teachers adopt a controlling motivating style toward students and how they can become more autonomy supportive. *Educational Psychologist, 44*, 159–175.

Reeves, C. W., Nicholls, A. R., & McKenna, J. (2011). The effects of a coping intervention on coping self-efficacy, coping effectiveness, and subjective performance among adolescent soccer players. *International Journal of Sport and Exercise Psychology, 9*, 126–142.

Ryan, R. M., & Deci, E. L. (2000). Intrinsic and extrinsic motivations: Classic definitions and new directions. *Contemporary Educational Psychology, 25*, 54–67.

Ryan, R. M., & Deci, E. L. (2002). Overview of self-determination theory: An organismic dialectical perspective. In E. L. Deci, & R. M. Ryan (Eds.), *Handbook of self-determination research* (pp. 3–33). Rochester, NY: University of Rochester Press.

Ryan, R. M., & Deci, E. L. (2017). *Self-determination theory: Basic psychological needs in motivation, development, and wellness.* New York, NY: Guilford Press.

Salvagioni, D. A. J., Melanda, F. N., Mesas, A. E., González, A. D., Gabani, F. L., & Andrade, S. M. D. (2017). Physical, psychological and occupational consequences of job burnout: A systematic review of prospective studies. *PloS One, 12*, e0185781.

Schaufeli, W. B. (2006). The balance of give and take: Toward a social exchange model of burnout. *Revue Internationale de Psychologie Sociale, 19*, 75–119.

Schaufeli, W. B., Dierendonck, D. V., & Gorp, K. V. (1996). Burnout and reciprocity: Towards a dual-level social exchange model. *Work & Stress, 10*, 225–237.

Shin, H., Park, Y. M., Ying, J. Y., Kim, B., Noh, H., & Lee, S. M. (2014). Relationships between coping strategies and burnout symptoms: A meta-analytic approach. *Professional Psychology: Research and Practice, 45*, 44–56.

Silva, J. M. III. (1990). An analysis of the training stress syndrome in competitive athletics. *Journal of Applied Sport Psychology, 2*, 5–20.

Smith, R. E. (1986). Toward a cognitive-affective model of athletic burnout. *Journal of Sport Psychology, 8*, 36–50.

Stoeber, J., & Otto, K. (2006). Positive conceptions of perfectionism: Approaches, evidence, challenges. *Personality and Social Psychology Review, 10*, 295–319.

4 Intervening to Manage Athlete Burnout

This chapter provides an overview of effective evidence-based interventions for athlete burnout. To do so, we first review the literature on interventions outside of sport, before talking through each of the studies that have tested interventions for athletes. We end by summarising the findings and outlining our recommendations for the most appropriate therapeutic modalities to reduce athlete burnout.

Interventions Outside of Sport

We begin with a discussion of intervention research outside of sport. This is because, like with other aspects of burnout research, there has been a much larger volume of work conducted. In terms of the types of interventions, in this chapter, we are interested in those that could be applied directly to the athlete (rather than the environment, which were included in Chapter 3). In this regard, then, we think there are two recent reviews that are worth discussing in context of providing an overview of the types of interventions that have been used for burnout that involved participants from a range of occupations.

The first review we will discuss focused on synthesising meta-analyses (quantitative summaries across studies) of randomised controlled trials (RCTs) of burnout interventions (Madigan et al., 2023). The review focused on interventions that had been used in physicians, nurses, teachers, and in workplace professionals more broadly. The focus was on RCTs because they provide the strongest evidence for causality by adopting randomisation of participants and including a comparison control group.

The review found ten meta-analyses that had focused on reducing burnout via individual-level interventions. Across these meta-analyses, interventions resulted in statistically significant reductions in burnout 35% of the time. It was therefore concluded that these interventions

DOI: 10.4324/9781003601098-4

appeared to work sometimes; however, there were many intervention strategies that were ineffective.

Importantly, the review did manage to identify interventions that were more effective. In this regard, the majority were cognitive-based therapies aimed at relieving stress. This included more traditional cognitive behavioural therapy (CBT) techniques, stress management, and relaxation strategies, and also techniques from the third wave of cognitive behavioural therapies such as mindfulness-based stress reduction (MBSR). The former techniques are based around changing underlying cognitive processes and patterns which in turn lead to more adaptive behaviours (e.g., Shafran et al., 2009). While the latter relates to the ability to stay attuned to the present in a non-judgmental manner, rather than ruminating about the past or worrying about the future (Kabat-Zinn, 2003). Interestingly, both approaches seemed most effective in teachers, nurses, and physicians. However, they did not appear effective in professionals (i.e., in the general workforce).

The second review we will discuss focused specifically on reducing burnout in students (Madigan et al., 2024). This time the review focused on summarising individual studies (rather than reviewing summaries).

The review found 17 studies (10 randomised controlled trials and 7 quasi-experimental trials), which included 2,462 students from secondary and tertiary levels of education. The studies had employed a wide range of interventions in an attempt to reduce burnout (e.g., psychoeducation, exercise, mindfulness).

When the effects were meta-analysed, there was evidence that collectively the interventions were effective in reducing total burnout (and that the effects could be considered medium to large sized). There was also some evidence that effectiveness varied as a function of certain factors (e.g., designs and intervention types). Overall, however, the strongest evidence was found for two particular types of intervention: rational emotive behaviour therapy (REBT) and mindfulness-based interventions.

In terms of effectiveness, REBT, which seeks to identify, challenge, and restructure irrational beliefs that are believed to underpin a negative pattern of behaviour (David et al., 2005), was found to be effective when delivered in person lasting between 8 and 12 weeks. In terms of mindfulness, more effective studies were those that were typically longer in duration (1–2 hours per week for 6 weeks), but the delivery format did not seem to affect their success (i.e., in person, group and, online were similar).

We are conscious that these reviews are based on studies that were conducted with individuals in a range of contexts that did not include sport. So, can these findings be directly translated and used to make recommendations for intervening with athletes? We think there is certainly some value to using these as a starting point. This is because they align well with recommendations that have been made elsewhere and also are supportive of approaches that are commonly employed by sport psychologists. Nonetheless, we think it pertinent to review the intervention studies that have included athletes before making formal recommendations for applied practice.

Interventions in Sport

We now move on to discuss the evidence for effective intervention that has been conducted in sport. As mentioned, there is a much smaller body of work in this regard. In fact, there have been just seven studies that have sought to test interventions to reduce athlete burnout. We think there is still much to learn from these studies, however. Consequently, we have summarised these studies in Table 4.1 and, so as to inform our recommendations, we now discuss each study in detail.

Dubuc-Charbonneau and Durand-Bush (2015)

The first study to test an intervention for athlete burnout was conducted by Dubuc-Charbonneau and Durand-Bush (2015). Their study adopted an observational design and examined the effectiveness of a 9-week self-regulation-based intervention in a small sample of eight athletes from various sports. The intervention was informed by the resonance performance model. This is a framework that is used to help individuals learn how to regulate how they feel, think, and behave to achieve congruency between their self and their environment (Callary & Durand-Bush, 2008). The intervention employed athlete and researcher discussions about topics such as perceived demands, resources, behavioural and emotional responses, preferred standards (e.g., how they wanted to feel), goals, preparation and coping strategies, and performance outcomes. Following 7–9 biweekly sessions, reductions in both exhaustion and reduced sense of accomplishment (but not devaluation) were found.

Moen et al. (2015)

Shortly after, Moen et al. (2015) provided the second test of an intervention for athlete burnout. Their study adopted a group-level randomised control design and examined the effectiveness of a 12-week mindfulness intervention in a sample of 50 athletes from a range of sports. The intervention had four phases. First, to train concentration and focus over long periods of time. Second, to practice individual meditation and to

Table 4.1 Studies examining interventions to reduce athlete burnout.

Study	*N Exp*	*N Con*	*Sport*	*Burnout measure*	*Design*	*Mode of delivery*	*Duration*	*Intervention*	*Main findings*
Dubuc-Charbonneau and Durand-Bush (2015)	8	–	Hockey (n = 4), swimming (n = 2), fencing (n = 1), and basketball (n = 1)	ABQ	Pre-post design	In-person, individual [athlete]	7–9 biweekly sessions	Self-regulation intervention	E and RSA significantly reduced over the intervention period.
Gabana et al. (2019)	51	–	Wrestlers (n = 27) and swimmers (n = 24)	ABQ	Pre-post design	In-person, group	90-minute workshop	Gratitude-based intervention	Total burnout significantly reduced at 4 weeks post intervention.
Liu et al. (2025)	29	28	Unclear	ABQ	Randomised controlled trial	In-person, group	1 session, 30 minutes	Mindfulness intervention	Total burnout significantly reduced following intervention, but no difference compared to the control group.
Luzzeri et al. (2020)	31	34	Cross country (n = 11), softball (n = 11), swimming (n = 8), track and field (n = 8), soccer (n = 7), volleyball (n = 6), basketball (n = 4), tennis (n = 2), and lacrosse (n = 2)	ABQ	Randomised controlled trial	Online, individual	6 sessions, over 2 weeks	Writing intervention	No significant differences between the intervention and control groups.

(*Continued*)

Table 4.1 (Continued)

Study	*N Exp*	*N Con*	*Sport*	*Burnout measure*	*Design*	*Mode of delivery*	*Duration*	*Intervention*	*Main findings*
Moen et al. (2015)	23	27	Biathlon, cross-country skiing, shooting and track and field	ABQ	(Group) randomised control trial	At home, individual	12-weeks, 3-7 times per week	Mindfulness intervention	DEV and RSA significantly decreased over the intervention compared to the control group.
Moen and Wells (2016)	25	32	Alpine skiing, cross country skiing, handball, biathlon, ski-jumping and Nordic combined	ABQ	(Group) randomised control trial	At home, individual (audio)	12-weeks, 5+ times per week	Attention training	RSA significantly decreased over the intervention compared to the control group.
Ofoegbu et al. (2020)	85	86	Para-athletes	ABQ	Randomised controlled trial	In-person, group [athlete]	12 weekly sessions	Digital story/ REBT intervention	All burnout dimensions significantly reduced over the intervention period compared to the control group.

Note: ABQ = Athlete Burnout Questionnaire. E = exhaustion. RSA = Reduced sense of accomplishment. SDT = Self-Determination Theory. Exp = experimental. Con = Control.

Adapted from Madigan, D. J. (2021). Diagnosing problems, prescribing solutions, and advancing athlete burnout research. In Z. Zenko & L. Jones (Eds.), Essentials of exercise and sport psychology: An open access textbook (pp. 664–682). Society for Transparency, Openness, and Replication in Kinesiology, licensed under CC BY 4.0.

train the change of direction and intensity of focus. Third, to train different mindfulness skills. And, finally, to maintain and to plan for unaided practice. The intervention included breathing training, body scanning with audio files, and reflective training diaries. Following 3–7 sessions per week, reductions in both devaluation and reduced sense of accomplishment (but not exhaustion) in the intervention group compared to the control group were found.

Moen and Wells (2016)

Building on their earlier study, Moen and Wells (2016) provided the next test of an athlete burnout intervention. Their study again adopted a group-level randomised control trial but this time examined the effectiveness of 12 weeks of attention training in a sample of 57 athletes from a range of sports. The intervention was aimed to enhance mental control and flexibility and was based on the work of Wells (1990). Using a mixture of at home practice and group sessions, athletes were taught to reduce self-attentional processing and enhance executive attentional control. Athletes were then provided with questions relating to the application of these ideas to their sport. A reflective notebook was used throughout. Following five sessions per week, reductions in a reduced sense of accomplishment (but not exhaustion and devaluation) in the intervention group compared to the control group were found.

Gabana et al. (2019)

A few years later, Gabana and colleagues provided the next test of an athlete burnout intervention. Their study adopted an observational design and examined the effectiveness of a single session gratitude-based intervention in a sample of 51 athletes who were wrestlers and swimmers. The intervention was informed by the concept of gratitude which reflects acknowledging a benefit received from someone else, or recognising the value of a general benefit to one's life (Lambert et al., 2009). The intervention consisted of a workshop where gratitude was defined, participants reflected on what they were grateful for, and why they were grateful for it, and reflected on what meaning this brought to their life. Immediately following this single 90-minute workshop, no changes in burnout were found. However, four weeks later, reductions in total burnout were reported.

Ofoegbu et al. (2020)

Ofoegbu et al. (2020) provided the next test of an athlete burnout intervention. Their study adopted a randomised control trial design and examined the effectiveness of a 12-week digital story and REBT intervention in 171 para-athletes. The intervention involved a series of videos that included stories of lived experiences of people who had battled and successfully coped with burnout. These videos were supplemented with REBT exercises focused on cognitive restructuring and re-education to develop rational perspectives about sport participation. Following weekly sessions, reductions in all burnout dimensions in the intervention group compared to the control group were found.

Luzzeri et al. (2020)

The penultimate examination of an athlete burnout intervention was provided by Luzzeri et al. (2020). Their study adopted a randomised control design and examined the effectiveness of a 2-week writing intervention in 65 athletes from a range of sports. The intervention involved four forms of writing intervention. This included expressive writing (aimed at exploring thoughts and emotions in relation to upsetting and pleasant sport experiences), reflective writing (aimed at gaining an understanding of these experiences), performance obituary (aimed at exploring how athletes would want their career and performances to be remembered), and photographic meaning (aimed at identifying and describing aspects of sport that athletes found meaningful). Following six sessions, there were no significant differences in burnout symptoms across the intervention and control groups.

Liu et al. (2025)

The most recent study examining an athlete burnout intervention was produced by Liu et al. (2025). Their study adopted a randomised control design and examined the effectiveness of a brief mindfulness-based intervention in 57 athletes (their sports, however, were unclear). The intervention involved a single group session that included 30 minutes mindfulness practice (focused on body scanning, using an audio recording) and then a brief discussion. While total burnout significantly reduced in the intervention group, there were no differences across the intervention and control groups.

There are a number of notable outcomes of reviewing this work. First, there is clearly a much smaller body of work dedicated to intervention in sport than outside of it. Second, unlike outside of sport, in sport, there has yet to be any systematic study of intervention types. Finally, and most importantly, although only a few studies exist, and the symptoms of burnout that were affected differed across studies, there is evidence that athlete burnout can indeed be reduced.

Recommendations for Intervening to Reduce Athlete Burnout

Now having reviewed the best evidence to date both outside and inside of sport, we seek to provide practical recommendations for the interventions that may be most appropriate to reduce athlete burnout. To do so, we first group our discussion based on the type of therapy that we think may be most useful when dealing with athlete burnout (i.e., CBT, MBSR, and REBT). As these are recommendations for qualified practitioners (e.g., sport and exercise psychologists), we then talk about other practical considerations concerning delivery (e.g., frequency). We also note that the choice of therapy will depend on both the experience of the psychologist and the needs of the particular athlete. We have provided a summary of these approaches and our recommendations in Table 4.2.

Cognitive-Behavioural Therapy (CBT)

CBT is perhaps the most widely researched therapy in the psychological sciences (Hofmann et al., 2012). It has garnered a significant evidence base, particularly in context of stress, anxiety, and depression, where its effectiveness routinely exceeds pharmaceutical intervention (Cuijpers et al., 2013). In addition, CBT is effective in reducing burnout in other contexts, and is effective for other disorders in sport, so it is likely it will also be useful for athlete burnout (see Gustafsson et al., 2017).

CBT focuses on identifying and changing unhelpful thoughts, emotions, and behaviours. The aim is to help the athlete to develop more adaptive thinking patterns and coping strategies to reduce distress and improve functioning. In context of CBT approaches for burnout, this most likely would reflect stress and burnout reduction. What, then, might a typical programme in context of athlete burnout look like?

In terms of duration, it is most common for there to be eight to twelve sessions, normally provided over a similar number of weeks (see also Smith et al., 2020). In addition to formal sessions (workshops or one-to-ones), there are homework activities designed to reinforce and support learning. These include diaries based on identifying and tracking thought processes, for example.

We have elaborated further on a possible CBT programme for athlete burnout below. This includes eight distinct sessions (see Table 4.2 for an overview).

Psychoeducation

The programme should begin with an emphasis on psychoeducation in relation to acute and chronic stress and burnout, which should be tailored specifically to the athletic context (e.g., Quintiliani et al., 2020).

Table 4.2 Recommendations for therapies to help reduce athlete burnout.

Therapy	*Description*	*Evidence*	*Practical recommendations*	*Example programme*
Cognitive Behavioural Therapy (CBT)	Seeks to change underlying cognitive processes and patterns	Multiple meta-analyses of RCTs outside of sport	8–12 weeks In-person delivery Homework tasks	1 Psychoeducation 2 Self-monitoring and values 3 Identifying negative self-evaluations 4 Exposure and dealing with difficult emotions 5 Challenging cognitive assumptions and bias 6 Cognitive restructuring 7 Dealing with Self-criticism and functioning under stress 8 Relapse prevention
Mindfulness-Based Therapy	Seeks to enhance the ability to stay attuned to the present in a non-judgmental manner, rather than ruminating about the past or worrying about the future	Multiple meta-analyses of RCTs outside of sport One RCT in sport	8–12 weeks In-person delivery Record heart rate At home practice	1 Introducing mindfulness 2 Mindfulness techniques 3–5 Mindfulness practice 6 Self-compassion 7 Mindfulness and athlete life 8 Relapse prevention
Rational Emotive Behaviour Therapy (REBT)	Seeks to identify, challenge, and restructure irrational beliefs that are believed to underpin a negative pattern of behaviour	Meta-analysis of RCTs outside of sport One RCT in sport	8–12 weeks In-person delivery Homework tasks	1 Understanding REBT 2 Identifying irrational beliefs 3 Challenging irrational beliefs 4 Self-acceptance 5 Beliefs and pressure 6 Beliefs and performance 7 Pragmatics of rational beliefs 8 Reinforcing effective beliefs

In this regard, athletes should be informed about common psychological and physiological responses to stress, as well as typical behavioural patterns that may contribute to the maintenance of burnout (e.g., avoidant coping). The rationale for the intervention should also be articulated to the athlete. An introduction to the effective strategies that follow in the rest of the programme should be provided as too should the evidence underpinning these decisions (see above; e.g., Clark & Beck, 2010).

Self-monitoring and Values

An important component of the programme should be values clarification. That is, athletes should focus on identifying personally meaningful change in relation to their life as an athlete and more broadly (e.g., what do I want my life to mean?). Doing so helps to provide a motivational basis for continuation and engagement in the programme. Athletes should also be introduced to self-monitoring at this stage. Doing so involves teaching athletes to identify personal triggers, maintaining factors, and behavioural responses to burnout. Athletes should be provided with information on how this can lead to a healthier understanding of the role of thoughts in burnout development.

Identifying Negative Self-Evaluations

Negative self-evaluations are negative thoughts that occur when athletes' rules or assumptions are broken. Athletes will tend to evaluate themselves in a negative, harsh, and critical way. Examples of such negative self-evaluations should be provided to athletes and their beliefs should be discussed. To begin to overcome these self-evaluations, athletes will begin to challenge them and help understand what is real and necessary over what is not.

Exposure and Dealing with Difficult Emotions

Exposure-based strategies should then be introduced. These help athletes confront and tolerate adverse experiences, particularly negative emotions (e.g., anxiety), that are common during behaviour change (Gustafsson & Lundqvist, 2020). A focus on avoidance behaviours linked to perfectionism and fear of failure would also be useful at this stage. More flexible athlete responses to adversity and adverse emotions should be the priority.

Challenging Cognitive Assumptions and Bias

Cognitive assumptions can often be rigid and unreasonable. For example, holding the implicit belief that I only have value if I win is unreasonable and likely to maintain dysfunctional coping patterns. It may have been that such assumptions were adaptive at one point but will likely be maladaptive under prolonged stress or failure. This phase of the programme therefore is about athletes identifying these patterns, recognising their unhelpfulness, and searching for more adaptive alternatives.

Cognitive Restructuring

To further provide athletes with the skills to think more logically and rationally, the next stage aims to reduce cognitive distortion (the preoccupation with negative stimuli). As a core therapeutic method, cognitive restructuring provides the basis to do so. Cognitive restructuring aims to help people reduce stress by cultivating more positive and functional thought habits.

Dealing with Self-Criticism and Functioning under Stress

Self-criticism can often exacerbate stress and induce feelings of inferiority and failure. Creating a better sense of perspective is important at this stage. This should focus on self-compassion and acknowledging one's limitations. This has the potential to decrease self-criticism and enhance self-worth. Furthermore, in order to enhance functioning under stress, athletes should be taught skills associated with assertiveness, providing and dealing with constructive feedback, and active listening. These are essential skills that can reduce stress in high-pressure environments such as competitive performance.

Relapse Prevention

The programme should end with emphasis on relapse prevention. This should involve reflection on progress and creating a plan for maintaining progress. In particular, athletes should be encouraged to identify early warning signs of heightened stress and build strategies to help maintain their thinking.

Mindfulness-Based Stress Reduction

Mindfulness is considered part of the third wave of cognitive therapies. It has its historical routes in Eastern traditions such as Buddhism, but has more recently gained support from various scientific fields such as neuroscience (Tang et al., 2015). Mindfulness, commonly incorporated as MBSR, has a growing reputation as an effective therapy. This includes for broader stress-related problems such as anxiety, but also in the context of performance (Si et al., 2024) and for burnout too (Suleiman-Martos et al., 2020). In this regard, there are studies in highly stressful occupations such as for physicians that attest to its effectiveness (Fendel et al., 2021).

Mindfulness is about present moment awareness, and accepting without judgement. There are at least three components to mindfulness practices that constitute a process of enhanced self-regulation, these are, improved attentional control, improved emotional regulation, and altered self-awareness (Hölzel et al., 2011).

In terms of mindfulness practice, the studies of Moen et al. (2015) and Liu et al. (2025) can help inform our recommendations. In terms of duration, it appears that brief interventions show potential, however, those interventions over a number of weeks (e.g., 8–12 weeks) have greater potential to be effective. This work also suggests that most sessions should last in the region of 10–30 minutes. In addition, this work suggests that the programme should be based on MBSR. Each session should be organised around a theme and contain at least two guided mindfulness exercises. Athletes should also be encouraged to practice daily meditation, including both formal and informal practices.

We have provided details of a possible structure for a mindfulness-based intervention below.

Introducing Mindfulness

The programme should begin by introducing athletes to mindfulness and present-moment awareness and it should clarify expectations. Much like for traditional CBT (see Gu et al., 2015), this should include providing an explanation of stress and burnout in sport and a rationale for mindfulness in managing these (including the associated evidence base). A programme will typically involve attempting to train one's concentration and enhance one's focus and to increase awareness of automatic stress reactions.

Mindfulness Techniques

The next session aims to introduce mindfulness techniques. These techniques are about developing body awareness and exploring how perception shapes experience. These should include identifying automatic responses to stress, learning to pause and respond with choice, increasing awareness of difficult thoughts and emotions and practicing non-reactivity. Techniques used include meditation with a focus on breathing and body-scanning (Hut et al., 2021). There are various publicly available audio recordings that can be used to guide aspects of the practice too (see for example, https://www.uclahealth.org/uclamindful/guided-meditations).

Mindfulness Practice

Mindfulness techniques are meant to be practiced frequently. As such, several follow-up sessions should focus on continued practice of the aforementioned techniques. These should maximise the effectiveness of the programme. We also advocate for the recording of heart rate (and where possible blood pressure) at the beginning and end of each session (Amutio et al., 2015). This is to provide athletes will objective information concerning the effects of mindfulness sessions and in particular relaxation and meditation techniques.

Self-compassion

Another important technique tied to stress and self-criticism is to focus on being compassionate. This relates to the ability to hold one's feelings of suffering with a sense of warmth, connection, and concern (Raes et al., 2011). Athletes should therefore learn techniques to increase their self-compassion, including, for example, self-compassionate imagery (see Gilbert, 2010).

Mindfulness and Athlete Life

The focus should then move to integrating mindfulness into athlete life. These sessions focus on enhancing mindful communication and empathy in high-stakes and stressful situations (e.g., pre-competitive performance). Work should then focus on transferring mindfulness into daily routines and performance contexts, for example using mindfulness or mindful walking during warming up practices.

Relapse prevention

Much like with CBT, the programme should end with a focus on sustaining practice and relapse prevention. This should emphasise the consolidation of learning and plan for continued practice and allow athletes to reflect on changes and challenges (including adherence, barriers, and benefits).

Rational Emotive Behaviour Therapy

REBT is a second-wave cognitive therapy introduced by Albert Ellis (1957). According to Ellis, beliefs can be rational or irrational. Irrational beliefs are rigid, extreme, and diverge from logic and experience (e.g., "I must", "I have to"). The main idea of REBT is that when faced with challenges and stressors some athletes react poorly as a consequence of *irrational beliefs*. Events are, therefore, not the direct cause of emotions and stress, but beliefs are.

As Jordana and Turner (2023) have articulated, the goal of REBT is to challenge, weaken, and dispute irrational beliefs and to adopt or strengthen rational beliefs. In doing so, the idea is to reduce unhealthy consequences and promote more functional ones. In sport, there is a growing body of work showing that irrational beliefs are related to mental health and performance issues (Jordana et al., 2023). Furthermore, REBT is gaining traction in sport psychology (see Turner, 2016). Challenging irrational beliefs that may underpin athlete burnout development (e.g., need for perfection) may therefore be worthwhile (e.g., Tóth et al., 2023).

In terms of recommendations, it appears that a duration of 8–12 weeks is effective for REBT. Commonly used therapeutic tools include disputing, Socratic questioning, rational self-talk, and cognitive rehearsal (e.g., Wood et al., 2018). As with CBT in general, REBT is also more effective with the use of homework activities including the practice of learned skills (e.g., Turner et al., 2014).

We have outlined a typical REBT programme for athlete burnout below.

Understanding REBT

The aim of the first stage of the programme is to understand the ABC model that underpins REBT. Athletes should be informed that when facing adversity (A) it is their beliefs (B) about the adversity that determines their emotional and behavioural responses (C), not the adversity alone. In the session, it is important that the athlete realises that it is their beliefs that are leading to stress and burnout, and that they can develop their ability to alter and control their beliefs, and thus control their emotional and behavioural responses.

Identifying Irrational Beliefs

In the next phase the aim is to apply the ABC model to the athlete, and to begin to identify irrational beliefs. This includes identifying activating events in sport. This should involve working with athletes to identify specific situations that trigger unhelpful emotions (e.g., pressure of competition). Then helping athletes connect their emotional responses (anxiety, frustration, anger) and behavioural responses (avoidance, withdrawal, rumination) to specific activating events. The focus then moves on to identifying irrational beliefs. This includes introducing types of irrational beliefs (for example, "I must always win/perform perfectly", "If I fail, I am a failure as a person").

Challenging Irrational Beliefs

The next stage is to introduce the disputing phase of the REBT approach model. In this phase, the goal is to teach athletes to challenge their irrational beliefs. This includes emphasis on whether the belief is logical, based in reality, and whether it helps in goal achievement. As a next step, athletes should be encouraged to reframe their irrational beliefs into more realistic and helpful ones.

Self-acceptance

The next stage involves helping athletes work towards self-acceptance. This involves emphasising that worth is not tied to performance or outcomes. Athletes should be encouraged to accept themselves as flawed but valuable, and this is the case regardless of performance.

Beliefs and Pressure

The emphasis should then shift to performance enhancement and pressure management. This is where broad psychological skills become important. Athletes should be supported to set challenging yet realistic goals and to emphasise process-oriented goals. Guided imagery and visualisation techniques are beneficial to mentally rehearse positive outcomes and build confidence. Incorporating techniques like deep breathing and progressive muscle relaxation will also help to manage stress.

Beliefs and Performance

In terms of performance itself, athletes can utilise mindfulness practices and establish consistent routines that cue them into a focused and confident state of mind before and during performance. Athletes should also develop positive and rational self-talk. Finally, athletes should focus on developing strategies for dealing with injuries, losing, poor performance, and other sporting setbacks.

Pragmatics of Rational Beliefs

In this stage, the focus is on pragmatics. Here, it is about helping athletes realise that their strongly held and frequently used irrational belief may not be helping and may actually be contributing to their performance issues. This stage is about helping athletes realise it is not necessarily external factors that are most important in burnout development but their strongly held irrational beliefs.

Reinforcing Effective Beliefs

Similar to the other approaches, the programme should end with a focus on consolidation and long-term strategies. It should aim to help the athlete better understand their rational beliefs and commit to these. It should review what has been learned and reinforce the importance of continued practice which should involve long term goal setting for continued burnout prevention.

Conclusion

This chapter has reviewed interventions to reduce burnout. In doing so, we have recommended three types of intervention for use with athletes – CBT, Mindfulness, and REBT. We have also provided example programmes based on the best available evidence.These recommendations are here to support applied practice and will offer practitioners support when dealing with athlete burnout.

References

Amutio, A., Martínez-Taboada, C., Delgado, L. C., Hermosilla, D., & Mozaz, M. J. (2015). Acceptability and effectiveness of a long-term educational intervention to reduce physicians' stress-related conditions. *Journal of Continuing Education in the Health Professions*, *35*, 255–260.

Callary, B., & Durand-Bush, N. (2008). A group resonance intervention with a volleyball team: An exploration of the process between a consultant, coach, and athletes. *Online Journal of Athletic Insight, 10*.

Clark, D. A., & Beck, A. T. (2010). Cognitive theory and therapy of anxiety and depression: Convergence with neurobiological findings. *Trends in Cognitive Sciences*, *14*, 418–424.

Cuijpers, P., Berking, M., Andersson, G., Quigley, L., Kleiboer, A., & Dobson, K. S. (2013). A meta-analysis of cognitive-behavioural therapy for adult depression, alone and in comparison with other treatments. *The Canadian Journal of Psychiatry*, *58*, 376–385.

David, D., Szentagotai, A., Eva, K., & Macavei, B. (2005). A synopsis of rational-emotive behavior therapy (REBT); fundamental and applied research. *Journal of Rational-Emotive and Cognitive-Behavior Therapy*, *23*, 175–221.

Dubuc-Charbonneau, N., & Durand-Bush, N. (2015). Moving to action: The effects of a self-regulation intervention on the stress, burnout, well-being, and self-regulation capacity levels of university student-athletes. *Journal of Clinical Sport Psychology*, *9*, 173–192.

Ellis, A. (1957). Rational psychotherapy and individual psychology. *Journal of Individual Psychology*, *13*, 38.

Fendel, J. C., Bürkle, J. J., & Göritz, A. S. (2021). Mindfulness-based interventions to reduce burnout and stress in physicians: A systematic review and meta-analysis. *Academic Medicine*, *96*, 751–764.

Gabana, N. T., Steinfeldt, J., Wong, Y. J., Chung, Y. B., & Svetina, D. (2019). Attitude of gratitude: Exploring the implementation of a gratitude intervention with college athletes. *Journal of Applied Sport Psychology*, *31*, 273–284.

Gilbert, P. (2010). *Compassion focused therapy: Distinctive features*. London: Routledge.

Gu, J., Strauss, C., Bond, R., & Cavanagh, K. (2015). How do mindfulness-based cognitive therapy and mindfulness-based stress reduction improve mental health and wellbeing? A systematic review and meta-analysis of mediation studies. *Clinical Psychology Review*, *37*, 1–12.

Gustafsson, H., DeFreese, J. D., & Madigan, D. J. (2017). Athlete burnout: Review and recommendations. *Current Opinion in Psychology*, *16*, 109–113.

Gustafsson, H., & Lundqvist, C. (2020). Cognitive behavioural therapy in performance enhancement: Using exposure and behavioural experiments with elite athletes. In D. Tod & M. Eubank (Eds.), *Applied sport, exercise, and performance psychology: Current approaches to helping clients*. London: Routledge.

Hofmann, S. G., Asnaani, A., Vonk, I. J., Sawyer, A. T., & Fang, A. (2012). The efficacy of cognitive behavioral therapy: A review of meta-analyses. *Cognitive Therapy and Research*, *36*, 427–440.

Hölzel, B. K., Lazar, S. W., Gard, T., Schuman-Olivier, Z., Vago, D. R., & Ott, U. (2011). How does mindfulness meditation work? Proposing mechanisms of action from a conceptual and neural perspective. *Perspectives on Psychological Science*, *6*, 537–559.

Hut, M., Glass, C. R., Degnan, K. A., & Minkler, T. O. (2021). The effects of mindfulness training on mindfulness, anxiety, emotion dysregulation, and performance satisfaction among female student-athletes: The moderating role of age. *Asian Journal of Sport and Exercise Psychology*, *1*, 75–82.

Jordana, A., & Turner, M. J. (2023). Perfectionism in sport: A rational emotive behaviour therapy perspective. In *The Psychology of Perfectionism in Sport, Dance, and Exercise* (pp. 328–350). Routledge.

Jordana, A., Turner, M. J., Ramis, Y., & Torregrossa, M. (2023). A systematic mapping review on the use of Rational Emotive Behavior Therapy (REBT) with athletes. *International Review of Sport and Exercise Psychology*, *16*, 231–256.

Kabat-Zinn, J. 2003. Mindfulness-based interventions in context: Past, present, and future. *Clinical Psychology Science and Practice*, *10*, 144–156.

Lambert, N. M., Graham, S. M., & Fincham, F. D. (2009). A prototype analysis of gratitude: Varieties of gratitude experiences. *Personality and Social Psychology Bulletin*, *35*, 1193–1207.

Liu, F., Yu, Q., Cai, S., Feng, Z., & Li, N. (2025). Effectiveness of brief mindfulness training for athletes' mood: The moderating effect of burnout. *Acta Psychologica*, *255*, 104960.

Luzzeri, M. (2020). *The effects of a meaning-oriented online writing intervention on commitment, stress, and burnout in collegiate athletes* (Doctoral dissertation, The Florida State University).

Madigan, D. J., Gustafsson, H., & Olsson, L. F. (2023). Reducing burnout in athletes. In I. Nixdorf, J. Beckmann, T. MacIntyre, S. B. Martin & R. Nixdorf (Eds.), *Routledge handbook of mental health in elite sport* (pp. 177–187). New York, NY: Routledge.

Madigan, D. J., Kim, L. E., & Glandorf, H. L. (2024). Interventions to reduce burnout in students: A systematic review and meta-analysis. *European Journal of Psychology of Education*, *39*, 931–957.

Moen, F., Abrahamsen, F., & Furrer, P. (2015). The effects from mindfulness training on Norwegian junior elite athletes in sport. *International Journal of Applied Sports Sciences*, *27*, 98–113.

Moen, F., & Wells, A. (2016). Can the attention training technique reduce burnout in junior elite athletes? *International Journal of Coaching Science*, *10*, 53–64.

Ofoegbu, T. O., Asogwa, U. D., Ogbonna, C. S., Aloh, H. E., Eseadi, C., Eskay, M., … & Otu, M. S. (2020). Effect of digital storytelling intervention on burnout thoughts of adolescent: Athletes with disabilities. *Medicine*, *99*, e21164.

Quintiliani, M. I., Imperatori, C., Testani, E., Losurdo, A., Tamburello, S., Contardi, A., … & Farina, B. (2020). Usefulness of psychoeducational intervention in chronic insomnia: An actigraphic study. *Journal of Mental Health*, *29*, 20–26.

Raes, F., Pommier, E., Neff, K. D., & Van Gucht, D. (2011). Construction and factorial validation of a short form of the self-compassion scale. *Clinical Psychology & Psychotherapy*, *18*, 250–255.

Shafran, R., Clark, D. M., Fairburn, C. G., Arntz, A., Barlow, D. H., Ehlers, A., … & Wilson, G. T. (2009). Mind the gap: Improving the dissemination of CBT. *Behaviour Research and Therapy*, *47*, 902–909.

Si, X. W., Yang, Z. K., & Feng, X. (2024). A meta-analysis of the intervention effect of mindfulness training on athletes' performance. *Frontiers in Psychology*, *15*, 1375608.

Smith, E. P., Hill, A. P., Mallinson-Howard, S. H., & Gustafsson, H. (2020). Stress, burnout and perfectionism in soccer players. In J. Dixon, J. Barker, R. Thelwell, & I. Mitchell (Eds.), *The psychology of soccer*. London: Routledge.

Suleiman-Martos, N., Gomez-Urquiza, J. L., Aguayo-Estremera, R., Cañadas-De La Fuente, G. A., De La Fuente-Solana, E. I., & Albendín-García, L. (2020). The effect of mindfulness training on burnout syndrome in nursing: A systematic review and meta-analysis. *Journal of Advanced Nursing*, *76*, 1124–1140.

Tang, Y. Y., Hölzel, B. K., & Posner, M. I. (2015). The neuroscience of mindfulness meditation. *Nature Reviews Neuroscience*, *16*, 213–225.

Tóth, R., Turner, M. J., Mannion, J., & Tóth, L. (2023). The effectiveness of rational emotive behavior therapy (REBT) and mindfulness-based intervention (MBI) on psychological, physiological and executive functions as a proxy for sports performance. *BMC Psychology*, *11*, 442.

Turner, M. J. (2016). Rational emotive behavior therapy (REBT), irrational and rational beliefs, and the mental health of athletes. *Frontiers in Psychology*, *7*, 1423.

Turner, M., Slater, M., & Barker, J. (2014). The season-long effects of rational emotive behavior therapy on the irrational beliefs of professional academy soccer athletes. *International Journal of Sport Psychology*, *5*, 429–451.

Wells, A. (1990). Panic disorder in association with relaxation induced anxiety: An attentional training approach to treatment. *Behavior Therapy*, *21*, 273–280.

Wood, A. G., Barker, J. B., Turner, M. J., & Sheffield, D. (2018). Examining the effects of rational emotive behavior therapy on performance outcomes in elite paralympic athletes. *Scandinavian Journal of Medicine & Science in Sports*, *28*, 329–339.

5 Considering the Future of Athlete Burnout

This chapter closes the current volume by discussing what is currently missing in athlete burnout research and, to guide future research and practice, what should be prioritised moving forward. To do so, we start by reviewing what others have recently said in this regard. We then focus on our recommendations for the future of research, before moving onto practice. We end by summarising thoughts on what innovation will look like for athlete burnout.

Current Perspectives on the Future of Athlete Burnout

We will begin by considering what other researchers (including our own previous views) have posited regarding the future of athlete burnout. These views have come from recent Special Issues (volumes of peer-reviewed journals dedicated to a specific topic) on athlete burnout. The first is from the *Journal of Clinical Sport Psychology* (Madigan et al., 2022) and the second is from *Sports Psychiatry* (Pires et al., 2024). We now summarise these two papers with a view to providing a baseline for how best to consider athlete burnout moving forward.

The first piece we discuss is a narrative review of reflections on the past 20 years and the future of athlete burnout research (Madigan et al., 2022). This review provided the thoughts and opinions of seven burnout researchers from a range of backgrounds and perspectives. The views in relation to the future of athlete burnout research and practice can be broadly summarised as: (1) further considering the social and motivational constructs that inform athlete burnout development, specifically with reference to the influence of the complex collection of individuals that form the social environment of youth sport, (2) more intensive and rigorous testing of athlete burnout theories to best scrutinise the factors that lead to athlete burnout development, (3) a call for a more intensive focus on longitudinal research designs, that use multidisciplinary teams and cultural inclusive methods,

DOI: 10.4324/9781003601098-5

(4) further consideration of recovery science and intervention within the research on athlete burnout, (5) the need for interdisciplinary, collaborative, team-based science to conduct large prospective cohort studies and multi-site randomised control trials testing athlete burnout interventions, (6) the need to broaden our understanding of the social factors that influence athlete burnout development to include the complex and impactful world of social media use, and finally, (7) to further understand and to publicise the impact of athlete burnout to key stakeholders (i.e., athletes, parents, coaches, administrators, sport psychology providers, sports medicine providers). Collectively, these views highlight some areas critical to future athlete burnout research and practice.

The second piece is a recent review by Pires et al. (2024) which highlighted five key "unsolved issues" concerning the understanding of athlete burnout. These five issues were: (1) to enhance conceptual understanding and measurement of burnout as a syndrome, (2) to better recognise and differentiate the myriad of potential negative mental and physical health consequences of athlete burnout, (3) to delineate the potentially complex relationship of athlete burnout with athlete recovery, (4) to build on the foundational knowledge of the relationship of athlete burnout with key social constructs, and (5) to develop effective sport-based burnout interventions for athletes.

Collectively, these articles highlight a key set of focus areas including ones that fit well into the considerations of burnout research (psychosocial constructs of interest, measurement, study design), practice (biopsychosocial intervention targets, intervention development), and innovation (knowledge development, knowledge translation, historically informed forward thinking) efforts that are well-suited to our thinking of the future of athlete burnout for researchers, practitioners, and participants alike.

The Future of Athlete Burnout Research

We now wish to consolidate our own contemporary views in regard to what needs to happen to progress our understanding of athlete burnout. Here, we start by focusing on four main research issues. These include the need for more longitudinal research, adopting of open science practices, awareness of the healthy participant problem, and continued emphasis on measurement. We now talk through the rationale for our focus on these issues, beginning with the need for longitudinal research designs.

Longitudinal Research

Athlete burnout research should continually improve on the quality and rigour of the research designs that are used. Foundational work in this area was informed by numerous cross-sectional studies (see Eklund & DeFreese, 2021 for a review). However, efforts to examine athlete burnout longitudinally continue. Recommendations for longitudinal work in this area are not new, with some of the earliest research in this vein occurring nearly twenty years ago (Lemyre et al., 2006). This work set an early bar for longitudinal research efforts which has been built upon by various researchers examining burnout in a range of populations including American collegiate swimming and track and field athletes (DeFreese & Smith, 2014, 2021), adolescent handball players in elite training academies (Isoard-Gautheur et al., 2015), and elite junior athlete populations examining the complex developmental relationships of athlete burnout and perfectionism (e.g., Madigan et al., 2015).

Such work continues to grow our understanding of athlete burnout. However, like all research, even if well designed, this past decade of longitudinal research has been hampered by two key limitations. First, increased consistency and rigour in research design and quality are needed. In order to examine changes in athlete burnout, studies with three or more data collection points of relatively complete data are necessary. This necessitates clear protocols for recruitment of large and diverse athlete samples that can be efficiently retained throughout the study's data collection waves. Combining recruitment efforts to include partnerships with sporting teams and organisations should be helpful to accomplish this goal. Furthermore, incentives are likely necessary to support athlete study participation and research protocol adherence. Researchers, therefore, need to be continually proactive and creative in seeking funding sources to support this important future work.

A second key area for consideration is the developmental window within which scholars should attempt to understand athlete burnout. More specifically, a key question is, when is it most appropriate to measure athlete burnout? Researchers have often examined athlete burnout within competitive seasons, systematically cutting off the final weeks of seasons when championship events are held (e.g., DeFreese & Smith, 2014). Whereas other groups have followed athletes across multiple years of their careers including both in-season (i.e., during competition) and off-season (i.e., potentially training but not competing consistently) participation. Though we do not feel strongly about any specific window for examining athlete burnout, we do feel that the lack of consistency of the time periods examined across studies limits cross-sample comparison. Notably, a reasonable scientific compromise outlining a "best-practice" athlete burnout assessment protocol for in-season and multiple-season assessment could help move this literature forward dramatically. Altogether, the future of the next 20 years of longitudinal athlete burnout research is bright if key limitations are addressed to build on the strong foundation to date.

Open Science Practices

Since the controversies surrounding the work of Bem (2011) and several "crises of replication" (e.g., Maxwell et al., 2015), open science and its associated practices have been at the forefront of psychology research. These practices have recently begun to be adopted in sport science as well (Zenko et al., 2020). Such work involves pre-registering study protocols (making clear what will be done including being explicit about expectations) and making data sets and associated data analytic coding processes publicly available. In addition, some journals now offer the ability to publish registered reports, where the study rationale and methodology are peer-reviewed prior to the commencement of the study. Specifically, if the study is then conducted as per these protocols, it is accepted for publication in relatively quick order, as peer review is then needed only for the results and interpretation aspects of the manuscript. These efforts serve to support researchers in carefully thinking about and planning their research. Ultimately, such open science practices aid in strengthening hypothesis testing, enhancing transparency, and helping to reduce bias. Work in this area has begun to adopt such practices (e.g., Glandorf et al., 2025), but concerted effort by researchers across the globe are required to help and support the transition to open science in the area of athlete burnout research going forward.

The Healthy Worker Problem

A major issue with studying burnout is the potential for healthy worker effects (Schaufeli & Enzmann, 1998). As is the case with studying burnout outside of sport (e.g., nurses, teachers, social workers), athletes experiencing burnout may be less likely or unavailable to participate in research than athletes who are experiencing few or no burnout symptoms. Accordingly, we think there are two primary mechanisms here that impact the recruitment of "burned-out" athletes for research. First, these individuals may have already left the sporting environment altogether. As noted in Chapter 2, attrition and dropout are notable consequences of burnout. Consequently, if these athletes have indeed left sport, recruiting them using current methodologies is unlikely to be effective. Second, and along similar lines, athletes experiencing high levels of burnout may not be interested in engaging in research. This could be directly related to burnout symptoms preventing them from adding "another task" to their sport-related activities or potentially resulting from perceived stigma about participating in research about a current mental health experience.

So, then, what are the best ways to recruit individuals with high levels of athlete burnout to participate in research? While we do not feel there are "perfect" answers to this complex methodological issue, we present a few concrete ideas for future consideration. For example, researchers can (1) actively engage with individuals who have recently left sport, (2) promote athlete burnout studies with de-stigmatising and inclusive language suggesting all ranges of experience with athlete burnout, past and present, are welcome and needed, and (3) adopt best practice engagement and follow-up procedures (e.g., fair participant compensation, inducements for participation in all study data collection points). Such strategies will help to promote the recruitment of and adherence of participants to the research protocol, regardless of how burnout symptoms may wax and wane throughout study participation. To gain a full and proper understanding of athlete burnout, recruiting athletes from a range of participation levels, demographic profiles, and burnout symptoms is necessary.

Measurement of Athlete Burnout

The future of athlete burnout research will also be unable to avoid the "elephant in the room" of appropriate and consistent measurement of the symptoms over time. Though not a pure consensus among all in the sport science community (e.g., Gustafsson et al., 2016), the Athlete Burnout Questionnaire (ABQ) is the most commonly used measure of athlete burnout to date. That said, however, it is always best practice to continually monitor and evaluate the reliability, validity, and stability of any psychometric instrument, especially after over two decades of research on an important topic like athlete burnout. Notable considerations for such work include assessing scale probabilities cross-culturally, examining how the face validity of burnout items may impact potential social desirability bias for participants, and investigating whether the current scale length (i.e., 15 items, 5 per burnout dimension) is best or if future scale development research efforts may help to identify an ABQ "short form" more suitable in length for prospective research and monitoring efforts (e.g., Casanova et al., 2023). Importantly, as articulated in Chapter 1, athlete burnout measurement was a historical crux for the proliferation of research in this important area and should continue to be re-visited and prioritised as research in the area goes forward.

The Future of Athlete Burnout Practice

Though we do not perceive the future of practice of athlete burnout to be altogether separated from research, we do feel that there are three key areas for consideration in the practice space going forward. These are the need for rigorously tested approaches to intervention, engaging stakeholders, and considering a move to a clinical diagnosis. We begin by discussing interventions.

Interventions

As attested to by Chapter 4, there are few studies that have systematically focused on the design, implementation, and evaluation of interventions to prevent and manage athlete burnout. We have made some recommendations based on the best available evidence both inside and outside sport (see Chapter 4). Given where we are in terms of understanding burnout, there has been no better time to intervene or further develop the means for intervention. Building on the approaches we have already offered, there may be multiple means to do so. For example, some evidence points to other specific therapeutic modalities such as acceptance and commitment therapy (Towey-Swift et al., 2023). Ensuring evaluations of such work are conducted is important, as too is ensuring the quality of such work from a design and methodological perspective (e.g., RCTs). In addition, as we have offered in Chapter 1, evaluating the monitoring of, and concurrent intervention for, burnout symptoms may also be worthwhile.

Literacy of Stakeholders

For interventions to be most effective, there needs to be buy in from all those involved. However, we feel that there is still a relatively considerable distance to travel when it comes to knowledge and literacy on the topic of athlete burnout for all key stakeholders. These include sporting organisations, coaches, parents, sport psychology and sports medicine providers, and athletes themselves. For example, it is common for those with significant influence, like coaches, to conceptualise athlete burnout as being primarily exhaustion-based and solely driven by training demands (Kroshus & DeFreese, 2017). Educational and knowledge translation efforts would certainly benefit from a focus on the true multidimensional nature of athlete burnout including the two remaining components (reduced accomplishment and sport devaluation), particularly given their recent links to athlete performance (see Chapter 2). This work should also include a more critical articulation of the link between athlete burnout and training load.

There are historical concerns that athlete burnout may be considered an individual "problem" rather than an organisational issue (Coakley, 1992, 2009). This idea is also certainly relevant to future efforts to broaden understanding of the athlete burnout experience. Important work in this area has been done via the spotlight on athlete burnout within position statements of notable sport-focused organisations and groups (e.g., Chang et al., 2020; Kellmann et al., 2018). However, more work can certainly be done using joint statements that involve athlete voices and educational resources available in formats beyond traditional academic and practice publications (e.g., videos, social media posts, embedded within long-term athlete development protocols). Such multimedia efforts mirror those utilised more recently to promote the importance of other athlete mental health outcomes including anxiety and depression. Doing so will only help to change knowledge and beliefs about athlete burnout and enhance our ability to deal with it.

Clinical Diagnosis of Burnout

An additional important practical consideration for athlete burnout going forward is a potential move towards a clinical diagnosis of burnout. Burnout was recently recognised as a psychological area of concern by the World Health Organization (2019) and appears in their Diagnostic and Statistical Manual of Mental Disorders as an occupational phenomenon. Likely considered as the first step towards a formal future DSM diagnosis, pushing forward for more clinical recognition of the importance of this issue would be a key step for athlete burnout practice. Following the path of occupational psychology seems potentially fruitful in that they have led the way in establishing this path for burnout outside of sport, the construct from which athlete burnout initially developed. To move understanding, recognition, and, importantly, treatment access forward, this step would be suitable and necessary for athlete burnout as well.

A Space for Innovation

We now end this chapter, and book, with what we feel is a bold statement. We think the area of athlete burnout provides perhaps the largest possibility for innovation in research and practice across any area of sport psychology. This is because of the potential to consider not only psychological but also biological and social antecedents and consequences. Such a biopsychosocial approach has been applied in other areas like injury (Brewer, 2007) and, as such, may have particular merit and usefulness in context of athlete burnout. The integration of biological (e.g., biomarkers), social (e.g., social networks and media), and psychological factors (e.g., depression), we think, will provide the potential for a high degree of innovation for athlete burnout work moving forward.

In a similar vein, the development of technologies to assist and advance research is key for future athlete burnout research. Developments in the assessment of salivary and blood-based biomarkers will allow for researchers to build on historical (Cresswell & Eklund, 2007) and contemporary (e.g., Glandorf et al., 2025) work in this space. Importantly, developments that reduce the cost and increase the reliability and ease of biomarker measurement will have a huge impact on the field. The prospective monitoring of biomarkers in active athletes would be a critical and important innovation to advance athlete burnout research. Similarly, technology that enables real-time tracking of training load and associated mood disturbances, in addition to life stress, would allow for a more complete picture of the demands that athletes face both in and outside of their sport. Doing so would also allow for the integration of athlete burnout more deeply within the broader field of sport science where monitoring and assessment of physiological factors is commonplace. We hope that work in this area continues to demonstrate the necessity for athlete burnout to be considered as an important issue for many if not all athletes.

Finally, and perhaps somewhat surprisingly, we feel that one way in which we can enhance innovation is for researchers to be more cognizant of the history of burnout and existing work that has taken place both inside and outside of sport. We think important advances in the field have occurred from borrowing concepts and approaches from the wider field of psychology. But to be really innovative, a knowledge of this work is essential. Working collaboratively with others who may not be experts in sport but know about other related areas or constructs (e.g., stress) would be one way to help do so. Innovation, therefore is not meant to be an entirely precious word, but one that looks both forward and backward in shaping a course for the exciting future of athlete burnout.

Conclusion

We have highlighted some key areas for future athlete burnout research and practice. We have also considered possible factors that may drive innovation in this area. We end this book then by hoping these guidelines and recommendations help to continue and enhance adaptive sport participation and healthy competitive experiences, and safeguard athlete mental health by protecting athletes from burnout.

References

American Psychological Association. (2017). Ethical principles of psychologists and code of conduct (2002, amended effective June 1, 2010, and January 1, 2017). https://www.apa.org/ethics/code/

Bem, D. J. (2011). Feeling the future: Experimental evidence for anomalous retroactive influences on cognition and affect. *Journal of Personality and Social Psychology*, *100*, 407–425.

Brewer, B. W. (2007). Psychology of sport rehabilitation. In G. Tenenbaum & R. C. Eklund (Eds.), *Handbook of sport psychology* (3rd ed., pp. 404–424). Hoboken, NJ: Wiley.

Casanova, M. P., Reeves, A. J., & Baker, R. T. (2023). Psychometric properties of a modified athlete burnout questionnaire in the collegiate athletics setting. *Journal of Sport Rehabilitation*, 32, 581–589.

Chang, C. J., Reardon, C. L., & Wolanin, A. T. (2020). American Medical Society for Sports Medicine position statement: Mental health issues and psychological factors in athletes: Detection, management, effect on performance, and prevention – Executive summary. *Clinical Journal of Sports Medicine*, *30*, 91–95.

Coakley, J. (1992). Burnout among adolescent athletes: A personal failure or social problem? *Sociology of Sport Journal*, 9, 271–285.

Coakley, J. (2009). From the outside in: Burnout as an organizational issue. *Journal of Intercollegiate Sports*, 2, 35–41.

Cresswell, S. L., & Eklund, R. C. (2007). Athlete burnout and immune function. New Zealand *Journal of Sports Medicine*, *34*, 5–11.

DeFreese, J. D., & Smith, A. L. (2014). Athlete social support, negative social interactions, and psychological health across a competitive sport season. *Journal of Sport & Exercise Psychology*, 36, 619–630.

DeFreese, J. D., & Smith, A. L. (2021). A person-centered exploration of athlete burnout across a competitive season. *Journal of Clinical Sport Psychology*, *15*, 89–104.

Eklund, R. C., & DeFreese, J. D. (2021). Fatigue, overtraining, and burnout. In I. Basevitch & E. Filho (Eds.), *The unknown in sport, exercise, and performance psychology: Research questions to move the field forward*. New York: Oxford University Press.

Glandorf, H. L., Madigan, D. J., Kavanagh, O., & Mallinson-Howard, S. H. (2025). Athlete burnout and biomarkers: An exploratory, longitudinal N-of-1 Study. *Psychology of Sport and Exercise*, *80*, 102870.

Gustafsson, H., Lundkvist, E., Podlog, L., & Lundqvist, C. (2016). Conceptual confusion and potential advances in athlete burnout research. *Perceptual and Motor Skills*, *123*, 784–791.

Isoard-Gautheur, S., Guillet-Descas, E., Gaudreau, P., & Chanal, J. (2015). Development of burnout perceptions during adolescence among high level athletes: A developmental and gendered perspective. *Journal of Sport and Exercise Psychology*, *37*, 436–448.

Kellmann, M., Bertollo, M., ..., & Beckmann, J. (2018). Recovery and performance in sport: Consensus statement. *International Journal of Sports Physiology and Performance*, *13*, 240–245.

Kroshus, E., & DeFreese, J. D. (2017). Athlete burnout prevention strategies utilized by U.S. collegiate soccer coaches. *The Sport Psychologist*, *31*, 332–343.

Lemyre, P.-N., Treasure, D. C., & Roberts, G. C. (2006). Influence of variability in motivation and affect on elite athlete burnout susceptibility. *Journal of Sport and Exercise Psychology*, *28*, 32–48.

Madigan, D. J., Gustafsson, H., Hill, A. P., Mellano, K. T., Pacewicz, C. E., Raedeke, T. D., & Smith, A. L. (2022). Perspectives on the future of burnout in sport. *Journal of Clinical Sport Psychology*, *16*, 75–88.

Madigan, D. J., Stoeber, J., & Passfield, L. (2015). Perfectionism and burnout in junior athletes: A three-month longitudinal study. *Journal of Sport & Exercise Psychology*, *37*, 305–315.

Maxwell, S. E., Lau, M. Y., & Howard, G. S. (2015). Is psychology suffering from a replication crisis? What does "failure to replicate" really mean? *American Psychologist*, *70*, 487.

Pires, D. A., Isoard-Gautheur, S., Madigan, D. J., Smith, A. L., & Gustafsson, H. (2024). Five unsolved Issues concerning burnout in athletes: An expert perspective. *Sports Psychiatry*, *3*, 39–46.

Schaufeli, W., & Enzmann, D. (1998). *The burnout companion to study and practice: A critical analysis*. London: Taylor & Francis.

Towey-Swift, K. D., Lauvrud, C., & Whittington, R. (2023). Acceptance and commitment therapy (ACT) for professional staff burnout: a systematic review and narrative synthesis of controlled trials. *Journal of Mental Health*, *32*, 452–464.

World Health Organization. (2019). Burn-out an "occupational phenomenon": International classification of diseases. https://www.who.int/news/item/28-05-2019-burnout-an-occupational-phenomenon-international-classification-of-diseas

Zenko, Z., Steele, J., & Mills, J. P. (2020). Communications in Kinesiology: A new open access journal from the Society for Transparency, Openness, and Replication in Kinesiology. *Communications in Kinesiology*, *1*, 1–3.

Index

Note: Pages in **bold** and *italics* refer to tables and figures, respectively.

ABC model 54
Abrahamsen, F. 43, 46, 52
absenteeism 12
Adams, J. S. 28
addictive behaviour 16
allostatic load theory 14
allostatic overload 14
Aloh, H. E. 46–47
anxiety 16
Asogwa, U. D. 46–47
Athlete Burnout Questionnaire (ABQ) 3, 4; Maslach Burnout Inventory *vs.* **4**
attraction-based commitment profile 33
attrition, as occupational burnout consequence 13
autonomy 29, 35

beliefs 53–56; irrational 53–55; and performance 55; and pressure 55; rational 55–56
biomarkers 18
Blake, C. 35
body image dissatisfaction 17
burnout: consequences of *see* consequences, burnout; defined 1–2; methods to measure 3–4; symptoms, frequency of **4**, 4–8, *7*
burnout prevention 33; coaching practices, changing 35–36; coping effectively with stress 34–35; perfectionism literacy 36
Byrne, B. M. 28

Cai, S. 47, 52
Chung, Y. B. 46
coaching practices, changing 35–36
Coakley, J. 32
cognitive-affective stress model of athlete burnout 29
cognitive assumptions 50–51
cognitive behavioural therapy (CBT) 42, 48–51
cognitive restructuring 51
competence, self-determination theory 29
consequences, burnout: outside sport 11–14; in sport *see* consequences, for athletes
consequences, for athletes 14–15, **21**; dropout 19–20; health 15–19
Coping Effectiveness Training 34
coping with stress 34–35
cross-temporal meta-analysis 6
Curran, T. 12
cynicism 1, 13

Deci, E. L. 29
depression 16
Dierendonck, D. V. 28
dropout 13, 14, 19–20
Dubuc-Charbonneau, N. 43
Durand-Bush, N. 43

Eades, A. M. 2
Eades Athlete Burnout Inventory (EABI) 3
Ellis, A. 53
emotional exhaustion 1, 2, 13

entrapment-based commitment profile 33
Eseadi, C. 46–47
Eskay, M. 46–47
exposure-based strategies 50
expressive writing 47

Feng, Z. 47, 52
Freudenberger, H. 1, 2
Furrer, P. 43, 46, 52

Gabana, N. T. 46
Glandorf, H. L. 15
Gorp, K. V. 28
Guillet-Descas, E. 19
Gustafsson, H. 14, 19, 32, 33

Harrison, W. D. 27
Hassmén, P. 14, 32, 33
health, as occupational burnout consequence 12–13
health consequences for athletes 15–16; mental health 15–18; physical health 18–19

injury, burnout and 19
insomnia 16–17
interventions for athlete burnout: outside of sport 41–43; recommendations for 48–56, **49**; in sport 43–47, **44–45**
irrational beliefs 53–55
Isoard-Gautheur, S. 19

Jackson, S. E. 26
Job Demands–Resources (JD-R) model 27
Jordana, A. 54

Kavanagh, O. 15
Serves, G. 14, 32, 33

Langan, E. 35
Leiter, M. P. 11
Li, N. 47, 52
Liu, F. 47, 52
Lonsdale, C. 35
low commitment profile 33
Luzzeri, M. 47

Madigan, D. J. 12, 15
Mallinson-Howard, S. H. 15
Maslach, C. 1, 2, 11, 26, 29
Maslach Burnout Inventory (MBI) 3; Athlete Burnout Questionnaire *vs.* 4
mental health outcomes, burnout and: negative 15, 16–17; positive 15–16, 17–18
meta-analysis 6
mindfulness 51–52; practice 53; techniques 52–53
mindfulness-based stress reduction (MBSR) 42, 51–53
Moen, F. 43, 46, 52
mood, burnout and 17
motivation, and burnout 14, 30

negative mental health, outcomes in relation to 15; addictive behaviour 16; anxiety 16; body image dissatisfaction 17; depression 16; insomnia 16–17; mood 17; psychological distress 17; worry 17
negative self-evaluations 50

occupational burnout, consequence of: attrition 13; health 12–13; motivation 14; performance 11–12
occupational psychosocial syndrome, burnout as 1
Ofoegbu, T. O. 46–47
Ogbonna, C. S. 46–47
Otu, M. S. 46–47

perfectionism-athlete burnout theory 30–32
perfectionistic climate 31
perfectionistic concerns (PC) 30
perfectionistic strivings (PS) 30
performance: beliefs and 55; as occupational burnout consequence 11–12
performance impairment, burnout and 20
performance obituary 47
photographic meaning 47
physical exhaustion 2
physical health, burnout and: biomarkers 18; injury 19; physical and somatic symptoms 19; physiological indices 19
physiological indices, burnout and 19

physiological symptoms 14
positive mental health, outcomes in relation to 15–16, 17; quality of life 18; satisfaction 18; subjective vitality 18
pressure, beliefs and 55
problem-focused coping 34
psychoeducation 48, 50
psychological distress, burnout and 17

quality of life, burnout and 18

Raedeke, T. D. 2, 3, 33
randomised controlled trials (RCTs) 41
rational beliefs 55–56
rational emotive behaviour therapy (REBT) 42, 47, 53–56
reflective writing 47
relapse prevention 51, 53
relatedness, self-determination theory 29
Ryan, R. M. 29

satisfaction, burnout and 18
Schaufeli, W. B. 11, 28
self-acceptance 55
self-compassion 53
self-criticism 51
self-determination theory (SDT) 29–30, 35
self-monitoring 50
Silva, J. M. III 32
Smith, A. L. 2, 3
Smith, R. E. 14, 29
social competency model 27–28
social exchange theory 28
sport devaluation 2
Steinfeldt, J. 46
stress, coping with 34–35
stress theory 26–27
subjective vitality, burnout and 18
Svetina, D. 46

theoretical models, development of burnout outside of sport: Job Demands–Resources model 27; social competence and exchange theories 27–28; stress theory 26–27
theories of athlete burnout development 28; cognitive-affective stress model 29; integrated model of athlete burnout 32–33; perfectionism-athlete burnout theory 30–32; self-determination theory 29–30
Toner, J. 35
Turner, M. J. 54

Wells, A. 46
Wong, Y. J. 46
worry, burnout and 17

Yu, Q. 47, 52

Made in the USA
Las Vegas, NV
20 September 2026

ebe46fa6-b083-4155-bc69-79f655a7ae40R02